Supervising the School Psychology Practicum

Kristy K. Kelly, PhD, is an associate professor and director of field training in the School Psychology Program at The Chicago School of Professional Psychology (TCSPP). She has supervised and trained more than 400 students, ranging from first-year candidates to interns. She is a licensed clinical and school psychologist in the State of Illinois and holds the National Certification in School Psychology (NCSP). She was employed for a number of years with the Northern Suburban Special Education District (NSSED) in Illinois, where she worked with children with exceptional social and emotional needs. Dr. Kelly teaches courses in behavioral assessment, consultation, practicum, and internship. Dr. Kelly's research focuses on supervision and training in school psychology, consultation, and family engagement.

Shanna D. Davis, PhD, is an assistant professor at Eastern Washington University (EWU). She was a practicing school psychologist and administrator in the Minneapolis public schools for 9 years. She has taught at the university level at the University of Minnesota, University of St. Thomas, and Chicago School of Professional Psychology. Dr. Davis supervises practicum at EWU and teaches courses in consultation, behavioral assessment, professional school psychology, and assessment. Her research focuses on early childhood classroom consultation and supervision.

Supervising the School Psychology Practicum

A GUIDE FOR FIELD AND UNIVERSITY SUPERVISORS

Kristy K. Kelly, PhD
Shanna D. Davis, PhD

SPRINGER PUBLISHING COMPANY
NEW YORK

Springer Publishing Company, LLC
11 West 42nd Street
New York, NY 10036
www.springerpub.com

Acquisitions Editor: Nancy Hale
Composition: diacriTech

ISBN: 978-0-8261-2938-3
e-book ISBN: 978-0-8261-2939-0

Forms and Handouts are available from springerpub.com/kelly
Forms and Handouts: 978-0-8261-2866-9

16 17 18 19 20 / 5 4 3 2 1

The author and the publisher of this Work have made every effort to use sources believed to be reliable to provide information that is accurate and compatible with the standards generally accepted at the time of publication. The author and publisher shall not be liable for any special, consequential, or exemplary damages resulting, in whole or in part, from the readers' use of, or reliance on, the information contained in this book. The publisher has no responsibility for the persistence or accuracy of URLs for external or third-party Internet websites referred to in this publication and does not guarantee that any content on such websites is, or will remain, accurate or appropriate.

Library of Congress Cataloging-in-Publication Data

Names: Kelly, Kristy K.
Title: Supervising the school psychology practicum : a guide for field and
   university supervisors / Kristy K. Kelly, PhD, Shanna D. Davis, PhD.
Description: New York, NY : Springer Publishing Company, [2017] | Includes
   bibliographical references and index.
Identifiers: LCCN 2016015494 | ISBN 9780826129383
Subjects: LCSH: School psychology—Study and teaching. | School
   psychologists—Supervision of. | School psychologists—Training of. |
   School psychologists—In-service training.
Classification: LCC LB3013.6 .K45 2017 | DDC 370.15—dc23 LC record available at
https://lccn.loc.gov/2016015494

Special discounts on bulk quantities of our books are available to corporations, professional associations, pharmaceutical companies, health care organizations, and other qualifying groups. If you are interested in a custom book, including chapters from more than one of our titles, we can provide that service as well.
For details, please contact:
Special Sales Department, Springer Publishing Company, LLC
11 West 42nd Street, 15th Floor, New York, NY 10036-8002
Phone: 877-687-7476 or 212-431-4370; Fax: 212-941-7842
E-mail: sales@springerpub.com

Printed in the United States of America by McNaughton & Gunn.

To all of the supervisors and the students they teach.

CONTENTS

Preface   *ix*
Acknowledgments   *xi*

1. Entry Into the Practicum   *1*

2. Developing Initial Casework   *23*

3. Foundations of Special Education   *51*

4. Working in a School System   *71*

5. Moving Toward Independence   *89*

6. Planning for Internship   *111*

7. Termination   *127*

8. Enhancing Training Through Collaboration   *141*

Appendix A: Practicum Candidate Evaluation Form   *161*
Appendix B: Practicum Training Plan   *171*
Appendix C: Consultation Skills Checklist   *173*
Appendix D: Psychoeducational Report Rubric   *179*
Appendix E: Practicum Agreement for School Psychology Program   *183*
Index   *187*

PREFACE

Every school psychologist-in-training completes at least one practicum during his or her graduate career. Practica are an essential part of school psychology curricula and critical for candidate preparation for internship, the culminating experience of graduate training. Despite the significance, there is little known about how practica and associated supervision are addressed within graduate programs nationwide. Although important accrediting bodies and professional organizations recognize the significance of practica and field experiences with some basic requirements, training institutions have been provided little guidance on this topic.

Supervising the School Psychology Practicum: A Guide for Field and University Supervisors is a practical resource for those involved in the training and supervision of school psychology practicum candidates, including supervising school psychologists, university trainers, and graduate candidates. The book is designed, in particular, with the field supervisor in mind. We present information related to supervising novice practicum candidates in the field and assisting with training in basic school psychology foundations. Field supervisors will find many ready-to-use resources in the form of reproducible handouts, example formats, figures, and reference tables and boxes. University trainers can use this text as a guide for designing practicum experiences, to assist with training and supervision provided via campus-based seminars, or for adoption for a course in supervision. It may be particularly useful for doctoral candidates enrolled in a supervision course and involved with the provision of practicum supervision of more novice candidates. Practicum candidates may also use this resource to enhance their supervision and training. Trainees will find many of the resources helpful in building their professional identity and applying concepts learned through coursework in the field.

Supervising the School Psychology Practicum: A Guide for Field and University Supervisors includes eight chapters that are organized to roughly follow the developmental sequence of a full academic year practicum, from entry through termination of the practicum. While not all practica are designed this way, we have included content that is relevant to the supervision and training of contemporary foundations of school psychological practice and address issues related to a wide range of practicum experiences. Topics addressed include case conceptualization across three broad roles (i.e., evaluation, consultation, counseling) of school psychological practice, the foundations of special education, multitiered systems of support, development of important professional behaviors, and internship preparation. Our final chapter will be of particular interest to university trainers and field supervisors, as it provides strategies for effectively collaborating across university and field settings to enhance training.

Each chapter is organized in a similar format, with a focus on the following key supervisory roles: (a) candidate skill development, (b) supervision, and (c) advancement and evaluation. The content aligns with the National Association of School Psychologists (NASP) training standards and is meant to be a step-by-step guide to training and supervision related to practica. Each chapter also concludes with a supervisor-to-do list to assist readers in applying the concepts addressed. The final chapter is designed as a special topic in practicum supervision and focuses on collaboration between university trainers and field supervisors, as well as strategies for addressing common issues in training, including problems with trainee professional competence. **Handouts and appendixes are also available for download and may serve as ready-to-use practical resources. Many can be used as designed or modified for individual use. Download from: springerpub .com/kelly**

ACKNOWLEDGMENTS

As first-time authors, this was a long endeavor and there are many people whom we need to thank. We would like to thank our families, first and foremost, for all of their love, patience, well-timed snacks, and advice. We would like to thank our former and current supervisors for being the models and standards for practice, as well as an endless source of good ideas. We would like to thank Nancy Hale for being supportive, positive, and always interested in our work. We would also like to thank Uncommon Grounds on Clark Street for being an accommodating and delightful work space and our reward on many Fridays.

I would like to thank my husband, Matthew, and son, Franklin, for sharing their time and support during the process of writing this book. The challenge was steep but altogether possible with your encouragement and understanding. I would like to extend a special thanks to two wonderful grandmothers, Nancy and Julie—your contributions are immeasurable. Finally, I would like to thank Shanna for her friendship, humor, and steadfast support.

—Kristy K. Kelly

I would like to thank my family and friends for being endless sources of support, good humor, and occasional, well-timed awe. I would like to thank my former practicum and internship supervisors, Nancy Knutson, Andrea Canter, and Scott McConnell for their life-long lessons. And finally, I would like to thank Kristy for being such a great friend, colleague, and inspiration to be better at everything.

—Shanna D. Davis

ONE

ENTRY INTO THE PRACTICUM

The start of the practicum for the school psychologist-in-training is an incredibly exciting time in professional development. In many training programs, the practicum is the first formal training candidates receive under the supervision of a credentialed school psychologist. Whether in an educational specialist (EdS) or doctoral program, it can be assumed that a candidate has completed at least 1 year of formal coursework in the foundations of school psychology and assessment practice. In addition, some training programs offer candidates other applied experiences (e.g., service learning, clinic rotations, research work) that help to prepare them for work in the field. Regardless of the training model, the practicum is often the first time a candidate is exposed fully to the roles and functions of the school psychologist in everyday practice. As such, candidates require a high level of supervision and support from field and university supervisors, proper orientation to the school setting in which they are placed, and an appropriate introduction to the supervision process. This chapter explores each of these activities as they relate to both the field and university settings.

THE SCHOOL PSYCHOLOGY PRACTICUM

The National Association of School Psychologists (NASP; 2010) *Standards for Graduate Preparation of School Psychologists* define practica as "closely supervised on-campus and/or field-based activities designed to develop and evaluate school psychology candidates' mastery of specific professional skills" (p. 7). Some training programs may require candidates to complete multiple practica aligned to a particular area of practice, such as consultation or assessment, while others have designed a more general field experience that covers a range of skills. Above all, the primary purpose for the practicum is to develop candidate skill and competency in school psychology domains and should not be mistaken as a way to deliver important professional service in the organization or school (NASP, 2010). While candidates in training undoubtedly add value to the working environment of a school and may provide service through the practicum activities they engage in during their training, supervisors should not view the practicum candidate as a key service provider and expect to "share the caseload."

The number of hours required in a practicum may vary greatly depending on the requirements of the training institution or credentialing process for the state. Doctoral candidates typically spend more time in practica-related activities as part of the training sequence than a specialist-level student. In a national survey of specialist-level school psychology programs, directors reported that candidates were required to complete a minimum of 414.75 hours, on average, during practicum training (Lasser, 2013). The number of hours required by programs ranged from 200 to 1,200 hours. More clear, perhaps, is that practica must be completed for academic credit and prepare candidates for the school psychology internship (NASP, 2010), the culminating field-training experience. That said, practica placements are most typically completed on a part-time basis (e.g., 2 days per work week) and occur concurrently with university-based instruction.

As previously noted, a practicum should be designed as a closely supervised training experience (NASP, 2010) and is likely to include supervision from both university- and field-based personnel. Who then is qualified to provide this supervision? Both the American Psychological Association (APA) and NASP offer little to answer this important question in their guidelines for training (APA, 2013; NASP, 2010). What these two organizations do offer, however, are more clearly defined requirements for the school psychology internship. At the most basic level, NASP requires the following for the school psychology internship: (a) field supervision from a school psychologist, who has at least 3 years of full-time experience, holds the appropriate state credential for practice in a school setting, and is a regular employee by the district or agency; (b) an average of at least 2 hours of field-based supervision per week from a supervisor that is responsible for no more than two interns; and (c) the majority of supervision is provided on a weekly, individual, face-to-face basis (NASP, 2009, 2010). The reader can review NASP's *Best Practice Guidelines for School Psychology Internship* (2009) for a more thorough discussion of the recommendations for supervision, mentoring, and collaboration during internship training. Although these guidelines do not directly address practicum supervision, we feel they should be strongly considered in the design of a comprehensive practicum.

SUPERVISION IN SCHOOL PSYCHOLOGY

Supervisors help trainees "bridge the gap" between what is learned in the university classroom and the practical needs of the field. In the professional literature, supervision in schools has been defined as "an interpersonal interaction between two or more individuals for the purpose of sharing knowledge, assessing professional competencies, and providing objective feedback with the terminal goals of developing new competencies, facilitating effective delivery of psychological services, and maintaining professional competencies" (McIntosh & Phelps, 2000, pp. 33–34). NASP (2004) extends this definition with a focus on improving the "performance of all concerned— school psychologist, supervisor, students, and the entire school community" (p. 1). To summarize, good supervisors *teach* their trainees what they know, *facilitate* opportunities for practice, and *evaluate* trainee competence and readiness for advancement in the field. Both the trainee and supervisor are afforded an opportunity for growth and are able to provide additional benefit to the schools and students they serve through improved practice. Figure 1.1 illustrates the components of school psychology supervision.

Understanding the roles of supervision is a good start, but having a framework for addressing these roles is equally important. A developmental model of supervision is particularly useful in conceptualizing how the school psychologist-in-training experiences growth in clinical skills and professional identity over time. Developmental models of supervision recognize that professional development is an ongoing process and that supervision should be integrated throughout the course of professional practice, both during formal graduate training and beyond. Harvey and Struzziero (2008) describe a model that integrates work from Stoltenberg and Delworth (1987) and Benner (1984) that indicates trainees pass through various levels (novice, advanced beginner, competent, proficient, expert) before professional identity is fully integrated. A trainee experiences shifts in both cognitive

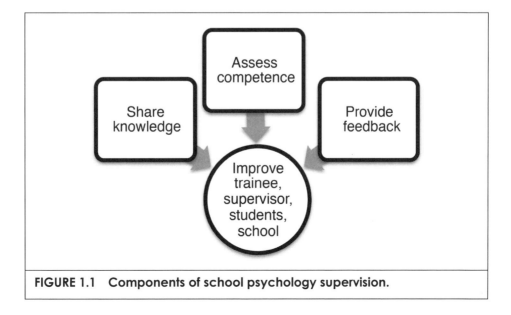

FIGURE 1.1 Components of school psychology supervision.

(concrete to more abstract) and behavioral (rule-governed to intuitive) development as they advance through each stage. Self-awareness in the professional role also improves as a trainee advances through each level. As shown in Figure 1.2, school psychology candidates enter the practicum with little to no applied experience in the various roles of school psychology and their training is consistent with what Harvey and Struzziero (2008) describe as a *novice* supervisee. *Novices* are characterized as being highly motivated, having limited self-awareness, and focused on skill acquisition. Given the multiplicity of the roles of the school psychologist, it is unrealistic to assume that candidates will advance much beyond the novice level of professional development during the practicum. Thus, the practicum is designed for school psychology candidates to gain a basic level of training in the roles and functions of the school psychologist. Depth and breadth of training should be expected during advanced field experiences (e.g., internship).

In these early stages of professional development, supervisees require highly structured and prescriptive supervision in order to control their anxiety and provide adequate direction in early activities (Stoltenberg, 2005). Novices benefit from facilitative (e.g., praise, reinforcement, attentive listening), prescriptive (i.e., provide specific input and direction), and conceptual (i.e., link theory to practice) interventions (Stoltenberg, 2005). The supervision activities and resources provided in this book have been designed with this understanding in mind.

A stage-based developmental model, similar to the one just presented, helps to conceptualize where the practicum candidate is in the overall sequence of professional development and provides some basic direction as to the type of supervision that will meet the trainee's needs. Process developmental models can help to provide guidance during more discrete and time-limited training periods, such as a 1-year practicum (Newman,

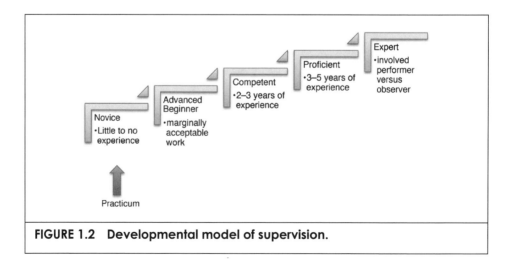

FIGURE 1.2 Developmental model of supervision.

2013). Harvey and Struzziero (2008) propose an adapted version of Alessi, Lascurettes-Alessi, and Leys's (1981) model for intern supervision that includes five stages of goal-directed teaching activities. Newman (2013) goes on to describe this as an "I do, we do, you do" approach to supervision, with supervisors modeling roles and activities ("I do") early in the training experience, working together with the trainee as skills improve ("we do"), and supporting trainee independence ("you do") toward the end of the training experience. We have adapted this model further to apply specifically to training at the practicum level and it is illustrated in Table 1.1. Each stage of the model is aligned to supervision goals and suggested supervision activities.

TABLE 1.1   Goal-Directed Supervision

Stage	Supervision Goals	Suggested Activities
1: Shadowing and modeling	Supervisee shadows supervisor to directly observe performance of professional activities	■ Introduce supervisee to various school personnel ■ Provide tour of school facilities ■ Orient supervisee to school and district procedures ■ Organize supervisee's observations of different classrooms and programs ■ Invite supervisee to attend various team meetings ■ Orient supervisee to roles and responsibilities of school psychologist in school/district
2: Observation and assessment of professional skills	Supervisor observes supervisee performing direct and indirect services, assesses supervisee developmental levels, and develops training plan with supervisee	■ Observe supervisee conducting a variety of assessments ■ Observe supervisee interacting with students, other school personnel, and parents ■ Observe supervisee interviewing students, teachers, and parents ■ Observe supervisee in basic consultation activities (e.g., teacher implementation of behavior plan) ■ Observe supervisee in team settings ■ Review current counseling cases with supervisee ■ Direct supervisee to conduct self-assessment of skill and experience in various domains ■ Develop training plan with supervisee for site that incorporates university and site goals and objectives

(continued)

TABLE 1.1 Goal-Directed Supervision (*continued*)

Stage	Supervision Goals	Suggested Activities
3: Guided independent practice	Supervisee independently performs tasks in which he or she has demonstrated competence and continues to receive more direct supervision for new skills	■ Assign basic case studies ■ Collaborate on supervisee's casework ■ Cofacilitate counseling group with supervisee ■ Assign individual counseling case ■ Collaborate on first full consultation case ■ Assign supervisee an active role on one or two teams
4: Increasing independent practice	Supervisee takes more initiative and responsibility for professional activities	■ Direct supervisee to conduct self-assessment of skill and experience in various domains ■ Collaboratively assess progress with professional plan and identify new goals for professional development ■ Assist supervisee in development of professional portfolio ■ Allow supervisee to lead case conceptualization on one or two case studies ■ Allow supervisee to lead group counseling for one or more sessions ■ Explore new counseling roles (e.g., new groups, individual casework, family support) ■ Facilitate school level presentation or activity (e.g., staff professional development, systems project, presentation to school team) ■ Allow supervisee to present casework in team meeting (e.g., individualized education program [IEP] report, problem-solving case)
5: Professional independence	Long-term plans for professional development are established	■ Develop termination plan with supervisee for site- and case-related activities ■ Assist supervisee in preparation for certification/licensure requirements ■ Conduct summative evaluation of supervisee's competence in practice domains ■ Assist supervisee in developing goals for internship (short term) ■ Assist supervisee in developing goals for professional work (long term)

SUPERVISION ACTIVITIES

Practicum candidates and supervisors alike often begin the year with a great deal of excitement about their work together. With this excitement, however, may also come some anxiety about how it will all turn out. Supervisees may feel worried about their overall performance and ability to succeed in the field, while supervisors may have concerns about their potential success as supervisors. While this anxiety is normal and should be expected, it can have a direct impact on the overall supervisory relationship (Bischoff, Barton, Thober, & Hawley, 2002). Supervisors should both recognize how these feelings may impact the process of supervision and also take care in helping to alleviate it in the early stages of the relationship. A thoughtful orientation to the field site and supervision process is an excellent way to address these early concerns. In particular, supervisees need to learn a great deal about how to enter the placement site, participate in the supervisory relationship, and take a more active role in their professional development. We discuss each of these activities in more detail.

Orientation to Placement Site

Formal orientation to the field site helps to set the stage for successful supervision. Even before the field training begins, supervisors should begin orienting their supervisees to the overall school environment in which they will practice. Like any organization, schools have their own culture and operating procedures and are often part of larger local districts. Supervisors can help supervisees feel prepared, welcomed, and connected to the school, even before they begin, by making efforts to help them learn more about the site. For example, most districts require individuals who will work in a school to first pass a background check and fingerprinting procedures before having contact with children. Supervisors should be prepared to help their supervisees navigate all of the building and district requirements to ensure a smooth transition into the setting. The roles and responsibilities of today's school psychologist may also vary greatly depending on the district needs, practices, and professional training of the psychologist. Given the limited experience of the practicum candidate, most will have a limited understanding of what the expectations are for school psychology practice in their individual field site. Orientation to the school psychology roles and functions in the field site, in relation to recognized practice domains (e.g., NASP practice domains), will help supervisees gain perspective about the work they will engage in during practicum training. A sample checklist for orientation to the field site is provided in Handout 1.1 and outlines activities that will help supervisors to prepare supervisees to connect to the site, understand the district policies and procedures that impact practice, and gain a clear view of how the field experience will contribute to their overall training in the field of school psychology.

HANDOUT 1.1   Field Site Orientation Checklist

Site Introduction
☐ Direct supervisee to read student and staff handbooks and review school/district website

☐ Provide walking tour of building facilities on first day

☐ Assist supervisee in completing all human resources paperwork, processes, and procedures (e.g., background checks, fingerprinting)

☐ Orient supervisee to building access procedures (e.g., keys, name tags, hours)

☐ Orient supervisee to workspace, resources, and office procedures

☐ Introduce supervisee to front office staff

☐ Introduce supervisee at first staff or building meeting

☐ Introduce supervisee via e-mail to all staff in building and explain supervisee roles and availability

☐ Direct supervisee to review information about school demographics and populations served

☐ Direct supervisee to review any school/district information about school performance indicators (e.g., test scores, parent involvement, programming)

School/District Policies and Procedures
☐ Direct supervisee to review school/district special education procedures and paperwork

☐ Direct supervisee to review school crisis plans and protocols

☐ Introduce supervisee to all school-related service professionals via e-mail and in-person

☐ Orient supervisee to all school teams (e.g., problem solving, behavior support, grade level)

☐ Orient supervisee to parent groups and resources

School Psychology Roles and Functions
☐ Review school psychology roles and responsibilities in the district

☐ Allow supervisee to shadow for first few days

☐ Introduce supervisee to other district school psychologists

☐ Introduce supervisee to peer supervision groups

☐ Orient supervisee to locations and procedures for student files and records (e.g., cumulative and special education)

☐ Orient supervisee to assessment and intervention resources

Orientation to Supervision Formats

There are a number of recognized formats for conducting supervision of psychologists, such as individual, group, peer, and live versus virtual methods. While individual supervision tends to be the most preferred (Milne & Oliver, 2000), supervisors are encouraged to consider using a variety of approaches to meet the individual needs of the practicing psychologist, supervisee, and site. We review formats here that we feel are well suited to practicum training.

Individual supervision

As noted, individual supervision is the most preferred (Milne & Oliver, 2000) and commonly used format for clinical supervision. Supervisors meet with supervisees face-to-face in regularly scheduled meetings each week to discuss training and casework. At the practicum level, it is most likely that supervisees will spend the majority of their time in the site with their individual supervisor, particularly in the beginning stages. This in-the-moment supervision, however, is not the same as formal individual supervision and should not replace this time. While much can be learned from working in tandem each day, much can also be missed in these interactions. Supervisees may not take the time or know when to ask for guidance and assistance with casework or may only get some of their questions addressed as the busy day unfolds. Individual supervision allows for thoughtful discussion of case planning and assists the supervisee in case conceptualization, a skill that is very new to the practicum candidate. Moreover, this format has been recognized as the method of supervision that provides the greatest level of protection over client outcomes and control over the quality of trainee work (Milne & Oliver, 2000). It is highly recommended that supervisors and supervisees schedule a formal individual supervision time in the first week of training and prioritize this time as busy schedules take over.

To maximize the time spent during individual supervision and assist the novice supervisee in learning how to participate in this important professional activity, we encourage supervisors to use a structured session format. This will help both the supervisor and supervisee to prepare, facilitate, and document what occurs during each supervision session. This will be the first of many supervisory relationships (e.g., internship, district administrators) the practicum candidate will have over the course of his or her professional career. Supervisors can thus promote supervisee development of important professional skills by teaching supervisees how to be actively engaged in the supervision process. For many school psychologists in training, the supervisory experience they have during fieldwork is the only preparation they have for providing supervision later in their careers.

We propose that supervisors consider structuring their sessions so that they are goal oriented, address opportunities for supervisee growth and advancement, and offer feedback about performance (see Figure 1.3). Teaching supervisees to prepare for supervision sessions by developing clearly defined goals in advance of the session helps to foster self-sufficiency as a trainee (Harvey & Struzziero, 2008). Supervisees should develop goals for supervision (what guidance do they need or questions do they want answered), feedback (what work or skills should be evaluated), and growth (what do they want to do next). The supervisor should assist the supervisee in determining what he or she wants from supervision and ultimately help the supervisee achieve these goals. Supervisors can facilitate opportunities for trainee growth by taking an active role in developing and maintaining the supervisee's training plan throughout the practicum. Over the course of supervision, the supervisor should assess how the experiences provided in the field are consistent with the student training goals (e.g., What have you done? What do you need to do next?). The final component, feedback, is a cornerstone for supervisee development and an important communication tool used to maintain or change trainee behavior. Supervisors should provide feedback to supervisees for three main reasons: (a) to facilitate skill development, (b) to change or "fix" problems, and (c) to respond to specific skill requests from the supervisee. Because feedback can be both difficult to provide and accept, the systems and formats for providing feedback should be discussed early in the supervisory relationship so that both supervisor

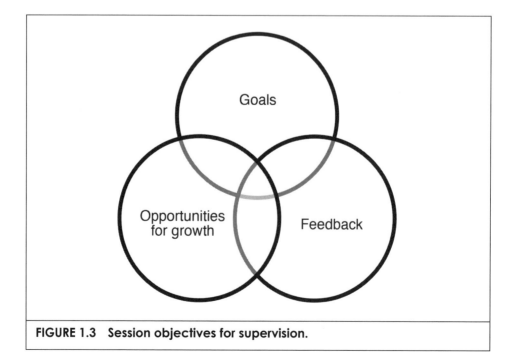

FIGURE 1.3 Session objectives for supervision.

and supervisee are prepared and more open to engaging in this process. We provide a more thorough discussion of feedback systems later in this chapter. An example session format for individual supervision, oriented around the three tenets discussed in this section, is also included in Handout 1.2. This tool can be used to both facilitate and document supervision sessions. Supervisors can complete the first page and use it to guide their discussion about casework, provide feedback, and document the feedback that is provided. The forms may be kept for reference in later individual sessions to ensure that the feedback is addressed in subsequent training and supervision activities. Supervisees complete the second page as an opportunity to provide the supervisor with feedback about the supervision session.

Group supervision

During group supervision, a supervisor meets with more than one supervisee at a time, and may use one of two different formats. The supervisor can provide individual supervision within a group setting, wherein the supervisor rotates to each individual supervisee over the course of the session. Alternatively, the supervisor can facilitate group support for individuals within the group or collectively address common issues for all members of the group. The group format provides benefits beyond individual supervision in that it allows group members to learn from one another and also provides a built-in network of professional support. Research has shown that this format is most effective when used with video/audio recording and experiential techniques (Ray & Altekruse, 2000), thus incorporating activities such as role-play, video analysis, and simulated activities may be helpful. Supervisors who are responsible for multiple supervisees may find this format to be a much more efficient way to provide supervision. This type of supervision is particularly useful when incorporated into university seminars that are provided on campus, where one supervisor monitors the training of a small group of practicum candidates that are at the same developmental level. Field supervisors who train multiple candidates at different levels (e.g., practicum students and interns) may also find this format useful in their work.

When using the group format, supervisors should also take care in attending to the stages of group development. Harvey and Sturzziero (2008) summarize a three-phase process. During an *initial stage*, the group leader establishes ground rules, orients the group to the structure of supervision sessions, and reviews expectations for the confidentiality of client and supervision work. In this stage, we feel it is particularly useful for supervisors to introduce and model a structure for group supervision so that case and fieldwork can be presented in a systematic way, helping the novice professional to develop early skills in both case conceptualization and supervision. Figure 1.4 provides an adapted format from Wilbur, Roberts-Wilbur, Hart,

HANDOUT 1.2   Supervision Notes and Feedback Form: Supervisor

Student prepared for the supervision session (e.g., identified goals, had data and information necessary to discuss cases)

0	1	2	3
not at all	somewhat	fairly well	very effective

Student objectives (list main objectives for supervision session):

Student presentation of cases and work was concise and allowed for focus on problem solving and consultation.

0	1	2	3
not at all	somewhat	fairly well	very effective

Student requests for feedback or guidance were specific and relevant to work in site.

0	1	2	3
not at all	somewhat	fairly well	very effective

Feedback (circle area[s] addressed):

Skill/Knowledge   Application   Dependence   Organization
Interpersonal   Accepting Feedback

Note feedback provided:

Supervision Reflection: Student

Rate the session on a scale of 1 to 5, with a 5 indicating a very successful supervision session.

1   2   3   4   5

Identify how the supervision met your needs:

Identify what your supervisor could have done to improve the supervision session:

Identify what you could have done to improve the supervision session:

STEP 1: *Request for Help:* Supervisee introduces a problem, challenging event, critical incident, or difficult case and identifies clear goals for supervision.

STEP 2: *Clarifying Problem:* Each group member asks one or more questions to clarify problem or case.

STEP 3: *Feedback:* Supervisor facilitates discussion around each supervisee goal or objective. Each group member provides suggestions to address the supervisee's goals.

STEP 4: *Reflection:* Supervisee reflects on suggestions and responds by indicating which will be utilized.

STEP 5: *Goal Confirmation:* Group discusses the process and confirms that supervisee's goals have been addressed.

STEP 6: *Supervision Notes:* Supervisor provides supervisee a written summary of the discussion and includes notes from session and additional feedback.

STEP 7: *Supervisee Evaluation:* Supervisee provides evaluation of supervision session.

Adapted from Wilbur et al. (1994).

FIGURE 1.4   Structured group supervision format.

and Morris (1994) that the authors have found to be successful for group supervision during practicum seminars in the university setting. During the *intermediate stage*, the leader provides active supervision thereby promoting a norm of structured and supportive feedback. During the *final stage*, the supervisor attends to the termination of both field and group activities. Supervisors should prepare for their group supervision by considering the life cycle of both the group and field activities.

Other formats

There are a few additional supervision formats that practicum supervisors may consider using to supplement individual and group supervision; we mention these briefly. Perhaps of most use is *collaborative work*, where supervisor and supervisee work together on cases and field activities. We have observed field supervisors use this method most often by working collaboratively with practicum supervisees to complete psychoeducational evaluations. This is particularly common when a supervisee has little exposure or experience to new assessment tools and methods and may benefit from observing the supervisor administer a test or analyze and interpret the results. Another format to consider is *team supervision*, where multiple supervisors work with the same supervisee. We have seen this used effectively when more than one supervisor provides supervision to a practicum candidate because they hold different roles (e.g., Response to Intervention (RtI) coordinator, counseling team member) in the district and want to provide the candidate with experience in various practice domains. University and field supervisors also provide team supervision to candidates when they work collaboratively to support the candidate through training. This team supervision can be enhanced with thoughtful planning and collaboration. For example, one of the authors asks each site supervisor to conduct an observation with her of each of the practicum candidates during training. A team supervision meeting is held with the supervisee, whereby each supervisor provides feedback and all three discuss how this relates to overall professional development and goals.

It would be remiss to exclude from our discussion on supervision formats the potential to also use various forms of technology in supervision, including phones, e-mail, and computers. Contemporary school psychologists work in a "tech savvy" world and today's practicum candidate is likely proficient and reliant on a variety of technology tools. Supervisors should plan ahead and discuss with their supervisees how technology will be used in their practice and supervision. Phones can be a useful way to communicate with supervisees when important situations (e.g., student crisis, supervisee illness) arise in the event that the supervisor is off-site or the supervisee needs to communicate outside of work hours. Supervisors should provide phone numbers (e.g., work, home, cell) to use for contact and also set ground rules for when and how to use them (e.g., hours of availability, reasons for contact, voice versus text contact). Supervisors who are unclear about these expectations may otherwise receive shorthand abbreviations via text late at night from their supervisee!

E-mail has also become a common and somewhat preferred method of communication in most workplaces. Supervisors may find it very useful to rely on e-mail to coordinate schedules and discuss general site activities with their supervisee. We recommend that supervisors be very cautious in how they use e-mail to communicate about the supervisee or the students and families they serve so that confidentiality is maintained. Supervisors and supervisees often share student casework via e-mail during the process of review and revision. At a minimum, identifying information should be removed from reports, student records, and written communications. As an alternative to e-mail, it may also be useful to explore the use of secure cloud sharing systems such as Dropbox or Box or utilize a secure district network to share case files and student information.

Supervisees may also need some additional guidance on how to communicate with e-mail in the professional world. For many candidates, the practicum may be the first experience working in a professional setting. Supervisors are encouraged to take some time to review how formal e-mail communications should look, either by sharing examples or having the supervisee practice sending communications to them. It is also important to direct the supervisee to create a signature line and appropriately note his or her status as a psychologist in training. Finally, it is worthwhile to also discuss expectations for response time and some common barriers to the use of e-mail communications, such as the increased probability for miscommunication. Supervisors and supervisees should proactively discuss how they will both prevent and address potential miscommunications (e.g., follow-up in-person) when they occur. For example, a supervisor may request a student meeting if a supervisee sends a lengthy and time-intensive e-mail asking for guidance with casework.

Videoconferencing has also been demonstrated as an effective tool for supervision (Chamberlain, 2000) and can be used in either individual or group formats. It is particularly useful when supervisors are required to provide remote supervision (e.g., location of site is a long distance from the training institution, commute times are lengthy). In a videoconference, the supervisor would meet virtually with one or more supervisees, meeting with them in real time. Supervisors may also choose to conduct site visits or observation through a videoconference format. This type of supervision is referred to as telesupervision and is defined as "clinical supervision of psychological services through a synchronous audio and video format where the supervisor is not in the same physical facility as the trainee" (Commission on Accreditation[CoA], 2010, p. 64). Doctoral programs that utilize telesupervision must have a formal policy regarding the use of this supervision modality and ensure that it does not account for more than 50% of the total supervision at a practicum site (CoA, 2010). Videoconferencing may also prove to be incredibly useful in facilitating metasupervision (e.g., supervision of supervision) activities for field and university supervisors. For example, a university-based practicum supervisor may hold monthly group metasupervision meetings via Skype with all of the field-based supervisors for a particular cohort of students to discuss supervision issues throughout the year.

Orientation to Evaluation and Feedback

Evaluation is a central component of supervision and critical to ensuring that supervisees are meeting the goals of supervision (Corey, Haynes, Moulton, & Muratori, 2010). Consistent with the NASP training recommendations for interns (NASP, 2010), candidates should be evaluated both formatively (assessed regularly throughout the training experience) and summatively (assessed at the end of the training cycle) during formal practicum training. Summative evaluation of trainee skills is typically directed by the university and is often accomplished when the field supervisor completes a form that assesses supervisee competence in various practice domains. Depending on the length of the practicum (i.e., semester, full year), the evaluation may occur once or more (i.e., midterm, year end) during the training experience. School psychologists in training are required to demonstrate both knowledge/skills and work characteristics relevant for professional practice in the field (NASP, 2010). Work characteristics refer to professional behaviors (e.g., time management, organization, flexibility) and interpersonal skills (e.g., cooperation, enthusiasm, empathy) that are necessary for work as a school psychologist. We have included in Appendix A a copy of the practicum evaluation tool used in the School Psychology Program at The Chicago School of Professional Psychology (TCSPP) as an example. The form requires field supervisors to evaluate professional skills and behaviors as they relate to the 10 NASP standards, as well as professional work characteristics demonstrated in training. Supervisors also make an assessment of the candidate's readiness for advancement to internship training.

While feedback by itself is a nonevaluative appraisal of performance, it is tied to the overall evaluation and advancement of the trainee. Meaningful feedback can assist supervisees in developing self-efficacy and an accurate view of their professional competencies (Steward, Breland, & Neil, 2001). While the benefits of providing corrective feedback are commonly known, this does not negate the fact that many supervisors struggle giving supervisees honest feedback. Some challenges include: (a) fear of upsetting the supervisee or damaging the supervisory relationship, (b) feedback that is too general and not specific, (c) an over-reliance on positive encouragement and lack of corrective feedback, (d) discomfort by the supervisor in giving feedback, (e) poor timing (i.e., too late), and (f) a supervisee being resistant or defensive to feedback (McKimm, 2009). Supervisors can help to prevent some of these issues by discussing how feedback will be provided and used at the start of the practicum and also by encouraging self-awareness around both the supervisor's and supervisee's approach and response to feedback. For example, the supervisor might prompt an initial discussion where the supervisor discloses comfort with the process of providing feedback and asks the supervisee to describe his or her experiences and expectations with feedback in other settings.

Supervisors are encouraged to find a formal system for providing feedback. Informing supervisees about the process and expectations for feedback will help to decrease their anxiety about the experience and prepare them to use the feedback more constructively in their clinical work. One method that supervisors may find helpful is the *sandwich method* (Daniels, 2009), where corrective feedback is sandwiched between two positive comments. This type of approach may work particularly well for the novice practicum candidate, as it focuses on using encouraging statements to deliver the feedback. A second approach for establishing a conversation about performance during supervision is the *Pendleton method* (Cantillon & Sargeant, 2008). The following steps are used: (a) the supervisee states what was good about his or her performance (b) the supervisor states areas of agreement and elaborates on good performance (c) the supervisee states what was poor or could have been improved (d) the supervisor states what he or she thinks could have been improved. Examples of each of these are provided in Box 1.1.

BOX 1.1   Example Supervisee Feedback

The Sandwich Method:
Positive statement: I really like the intervention you chose.
Corrective statement: I noticed that the student was not given a chance to try the task independently. Perhaps we could find a way to incorporate this into your current plan.
Positive statement: You seemed to have a great rapport with the student.

Pendleton Method:
Supervisor: "It's time for your midyear evaluation. We're going to use a model in which I will have you share what you think is going well, and then I will share. I will then have you state what you think you could improve and then I will share."
Supervisee: "Ok, sounds good. Well, I think I have done a good job getting my reports finished on time. I have incorporated your feedback and have integrated them more than I did in the beginning of the year. I have been working really hard in the resource classroom to help with Curriculum Based Measurement (CBM) progress monitoring and have enjoyed my social skills group."
Supervisor: "I agree. I have seen an improvement in your reports. I also know that Ms. Brown really appreciates your help and has really learned how to get progress monitoring up and running. You have done a nice job planning your group and the students seem excited to come each week. What are some things you think you could improve?"
Supervisee: "Well, I think I could do a better job with follow through. I notice Mr. Fredrickson didn't respond about the plan for Charlie. I need to make sure to follow up with him. I could also run my group a little more smoothly. Sometimes the students talk out and do not follow directions."
Supervisor: "Great ideas and reflection. It is great to follow up with teachers. I would agree that when you give something to a teacher or ask him or her to implement a plan, you need to follow up immediately for the first few weeks until it is up and running. For your group, the management is always tough. Have you considered an incentive system? We can work on this. I would like to see some kind of outcome measure to know if it is helping. Overall, you have offered a nice reflection. Let's follow up next week to see how these new ideas work out for you."

Feedback is also bidirectional (McKimm, 2009) and supervisors are encouraged to seek feedback from supervisees about their experiences in supervision. Supervisors should frequently assess how well their methods of supervision are meeting the supervisees' needs and whether adjustments should be made in order to better support training. Supervisees who are provided regular opportunities to provide feedback to their supervisors will find it less challenging to address potential conflicts that may arise during the supervisory relationship. Incorporating two-way feedback into supervision is an excellent way to teach these important professional skills to the novice trainee. It will also likely be a much more pleasant experience for both!

Development of Training Plan

A thoughtful orientation should also include the development of a plan that documents supervisee goals and activities for the training period. A training plan is a written document and can serve as a contract between the field and university supervisors and supervisee and is a great tool for ensuring goal attainment over the course of training. It is important to remember that the school psychology practicum candidate is often enrolled in courses on campus while completing the part-time field training experience. As such, practicum candidates often have to manage field-based training requirements from course instructors (i.e., applied assignments), practicum seminar leaders (i.e., seminar assignments), and field supervisors (i.e., unique activities related to the field site). While these experiences are all essential to the growth and development of the candidate, having multiple supervisors and expectations can also lead to miscommunication and conflict without thoughtful coordination. It is recommended that supervisors collaborate with their supervisees to develop a training plan that will be monitored over the course of the practicum.

A great place to start is to prompt the supervisee to document all of the university requirements he or she will need to complete in the field site. The field supervisor and supervisee can discuss both the feasibility of facilitating university expectations and ways they can be accomplished in the field site (e.g., assign casework and roles). If conflicts arise during these initial discussions, the university-based supervisor can be consulted for problem solving and assistance. The field supervisor should then offer input about the types of experiences and activities he or she feels are unique to the training site and beneficial for the student. The field supervisor and supervisee can determine which activities they will add to the plan. Finally, the field and university supervisors can prompt the supervisee to complete a self-assessment of his or her skills and interests in the field. Encouraging trainees to routinely appraise and correct their own performance helps them to develop skills for lifelong professional development (Cantillon & Sargeant, 2008). In our work, we have observed this done with very informal (e.g., general reflection upon skill and abilities) and more formal (e.g., review of skills and abilities in 10 NASP domains, inventories) approaches. One suggestion is to have the supervisees self-evaluate skills and abilities with the formal evaluation tool that will be used to assess competencies during the training experience. Upon completion of the self-assessment, supervisees can develop a few feasible goals they have for their own professional development.

Supervisees may find using the *SMART* method (Doran, 1981) useful when writing goals for the training plan. Goals should be written so that they are *specific, measurable, attainable, realistic*, and *time-bound*. An example goal for the practicum training plan might state, "Co-lead one 8-week social-skills group by April." This goal provides specific (8-week social skills group) information about the candidate behaviors (co-lead a group) that will be attained by the end of the practicum training period (time-bound). It is attainable, realistic, and easily measured through observation and documentation. Once an initial plan has been drafted, all three parties (field and university supervisors and supervisee) should review the plan for final revisions and each place a formal signature on the document as an agreement for training. An example training plan is included in Appendix B.

SUMMARY

School psychologists who supervise the practicum candidate are in a unique position to help train candidates that are novices in the field and are often completing their very first field training experience. Practicum candidates require supervision that is highly structured, provides a great deal of direction, and offers a high level of encouragement and support. Supervisors can help to set the stage for a successful supervisory relationship by thoroughly orienting the practicum candidate to the field site and the supervision process. Thoughtful orientation includes an introduction to the placement site, supervision formats that will be used during the training experience, procedures for trainee evaluation and feedback, and concludes with the development of a formal training plan. Supervisors should also encourage active supervisee participation in the supervision process and professional development by incorporating activities that promote self-assessment and reflection. Taking time to establish the routines, procedures, and expectations for supervision in the early days of the supervisory relationship helps to promote positive outcomes for the supervisee, supervisor(s), and the students, families, and schools they serve.

SUPERVISOR TO-DO LIST

☐ Orient supervisee to field site

☐ Orient supervisee to supervision formats (e.g., individual, group, other) and procedures

☐ Orient supervisee to evaluation and feedback methods, including timelines and procedures

☐ Develop a training plan for field activities

☐ Prompt supervisee to complete a self-assessment of current competencies

REFERENCES

Alessi, G. J., Lascurettes-Alessi, K. J., & Leys, W. L. (1981). Internships in school psychology: Supervision issues. *School Psychology Review, 10,* 461–469. doi:10.1177/0143034301223004

American Psychological Association. (2013). *Guidelines and principles for accreditation of programs in professional psychology.* Washington, DC: Office of Program Consultation and Accreditation.

Bischoff, R. J., Barton, M., Thober, J., & Hawley, R. (2002). Events and experiences impacting the development of clinical self-confidence: A study of the first year of client contact. *Journal of Marital and Family Therapy, 28*(3), 371–382.

Benner, P. (1984). *From novice to expert: Excellence and power in clinical nursing practice.* Melno Park, CA: Addison-Wesley. doi:10.1002/nur.4770080119

Cantillon, P., & Sargeant, J. (2008). Giving feedback in clinical settings. *British Medical Journal (International Edition), 337*(7681), 1292–1294.

Chamberlain, J. (2000). Point, click, and learn: Educators exhibited the cutting-edge technology they're using to enhance their classrooms. *Monitor on Psychology, 31*(9), 56–57.

Commission on Accreditation. (2010). *Commission on Accreditation implementing regulations Section C: IRs Related to the guidelines and principles.* Washington, DC: American Psychological Association.

Corey, G., Haynes, R., Moulton, P., & Muratori, M. (2010). *Clinical supervision in the helping professions: A practical guide* (2nd ed.). Alexandria, VA: American Counseling Association.

Daniels, A. C. (2009). *Oops! 13 management practices that waste time and money (and what to do instead).* Atlanta, GA: Performance Management Publications.

Doran, G. T. (1981). There's a S.M.A.R.T. way to write management goals and objectives. *Management Review,* (AMA FORUM) 70(11): 35–36.

Harvey, V. S., & Struzziero, J. A. (2008). *Professional development and supervision of school psychologists: From intern to expert* (2nd ed.). Thousand Oaks, CA: Corwin Press and National Association of School Psychologists.

Lasser, J. (2013). *Internship and practicum hours per semester* (Data file). Retrieved from https://docs.google.com/spreadsheet/ccc?key=0AqoXyD0HMgrFdHU2dDRHLUQ5VWdiVGZYMXVSUXU0aFE&usp=sharing

McIntosh, D. E., & Phelps, L. (2000). Supervision in school psychology: Where will the future take us? *Psychology in the Schools, 37*(1), 33–38. doi:10.1002/(SICI)1520-6807(200001)37:1

McKimm, J. (2009). Giving effective feedback. *British Journal of Hospital Medicine (London, England, 2005)*, *70*(3), 158–161.

Milne, D. L., & Oliver, V. (2000). Flexible formats of clinical supervision: Description, evaluation, and implementation. *Journal of Mental Health*, *9*, 291–304.

National Association of School Psychologists. (2004). *Position statement on supervision in school psychology.* Retrieved April 15, 2015, from http://www.nasponline.org/about_nasp/positionpapers/supervsion.pdf

National Association of School Psychologists. (2009). *Best practice guidelines for school psychology internship.* Bethesda, MD: Author.

National Association of School Psychologists (2010). *Standards for the graduate preparation of school psychologists.* Bethesda, MD: Author.

Newman, D. S. (2013). *Demystifying the school psychology internship: A dynamic guide for interns and supervisors.* New York, NY: Routledge.

Ray, D., & Altekruse, M. (2000). Effectiveness of group supervision versus combined group and individual supervision. *Counselor Education and Supervision*, *40*(9), 19–30.

Steward, R. J., Breland, A., & Neil, D. M. (2001). Novice supervisees' self-evaluations and their perceptions of supervisor style. *Counselor Education and Supervision*, *41*(12), 131–140.

Stoltenberg, C. D. (2005). Enhancing professional competence through developmental approaches to supervision. *American Psychologist*, *60*(8), 857–864.

Stoltenberg, C. D., & Delworth, U. (1987). *Supervising counselors and therapists: A developmental approach.* San Francisco, CA: Jossey-Bass.

Wilbur, M. P., Roberts-Wilbur, J., Hart, G. M., Morris, J. R. (1994). Structured group supervision (SGS): A pilot study. *Counselor Education and Supervision*, *33*, 262–279.

TWO

DEVELOPING INITIAL CASEWORK

Case consultation is perhaps the most common and popular form of supervision used in the training of psychologists. During case consultation, supervisees present client work in individual or group supervision sessions in order to obtain guidance in service delivery. School psychologists serve a variety of clients in school settings, including students, parents, teachers, and schools or districts as entire organizations. The novice school psychologist-in-training requires a great deal of support in learning how to conceptualize casework for a variety of clients and through a variety of roles (e.g., assessment, consultation, counseling).

Practicum candidates often enter the field with very limited casework experience. Campus-based activities may include simulated casework or limited applied experiences. For example, an instructor may require trainees to practice various components required for a functional assessment (e.g., behavioral observation, teacher interview) as part of a course on behavioral assessment. Often, candidates obtain this practice with "volunteer clients" that are not representative (e.g., typically developing, limited demographic) of the clients they will serve in the field. At best, training programs may afford trainees an opportunity to provide assessments and/or work with clients through a campus-based clinic. It should also not be assumed that a trainee has received formal instruction in particular areas, as practicum candidates are commonly enrolled in coursework during practice. One of the primary roles of the practicum supervisor, therefore, is development and attention to the trainee's ability to conceptualize service delivery in response to client needs over time. This chapter explores supervision activities to help the school psychology practicum candidate develop skills in case conceptualization across three main roles of school psychology (assessment, consultation, and counseling).

CASE CONCEPTUALIZATION FOR CASE STUDY EVALUATION

Contemporary school psychologists wear many hats and are trained to provide a variety of services, including assessment, counseling, consultation, and systems change, to name a few. Regardless of the expanding role of the school psychologist, professional identity is still largely tied to evaluation of student eligibility for special education. In a recent national study of the field (Castillo, Curtis, & Gelley, 2012), school psychologists reported that nearly 60% of their time is spent in special education activities despite an overall decrease in the number of special education evaluations and reevaluations. In fact, school psychologists reported dedicating 47% of their time conducting psychoeducational case studies (Castillo et al., 2012), suggesting that evaluation work remains a primary role in the field.

While it is essential to support trainee case conceptualization across various school psychological roles, it is a reality that trainees observe their supervisors conducting evaluations often and are likely involved in case study work early in the practicum. As such, we focus our initial discussion on case conceptualization to activities related to psychoeducational evaluations. After addressing supervision activities related to case conceptualization from a broad perspective, we focus on three main case study components: (a) development of the student referral, (b) identification of an assessment plan linked to presenting concerns, and (c) the design of interventions that are tied to assessment data. Figure 2.1 helps to illustrate the link between these various stages of case conceptualization. A discussion of case conceptualization activities for supporting trainee experience with consultation and counseling activities is then explored.

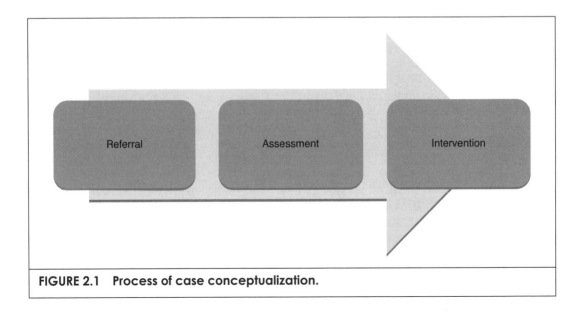

FIGURE 2.1   Process of case conceptualization.

Supervision Activities for Case Conceptualization in Case Study Evaluation

Practicum candidates require support both in terms of how they approach their work with clients and how they seek supervision and consultation. That is, candidates should first understand there is a general framework that guides their work from referral to intervention and that it is essential that they follow this process in order to provide meaningful service. It is not uncommon for eager practicum candidates to want to jump straight to intervention planning when teachers and parents express concern and request assistance for a student. Supervisors should expect to temper this enthusiasm by teaching their supervisees to follow a structured approach to client casework, such as the one depicted in Figure 2.1. An excellent introductory activity is to assign the supervisee a few case vignettes for review. Supervisors can ask supervisees to identify relevant information in the case vignettes that would be included in various case study components (e.g., referral, assessment, intervention) for practice. Or the supervisor may use simulated case scenarios to test and develop candidate skill. For example, a university supervisor may provide some basic background and referral information about a student and ask supervisees to identify an appropriate assessment plan for the evaluation. Site supervisors can use old casework for these activities as well.

Once the supervisee is comfortable with the case conceptualization process, live cases may be assigned. Novice trainees should be assigned less complicated cases in the early stages of training and move to more advanced casework as they demonstrate skill in the field. Practicum candidates will require close supervision and monitoring of their early cases and can easily get lost in case details. We often find that supervisees struggle to highlight the important pieces of case information when discussing casework and get sidetracked by tangential stories or stuck on specific pieces of information. The end result is a long unfocused discussion about the client or situation, with very little time to discuss what the trainee will do next with the case. To improve the efficiency and quality of supervision, we recommend that supervisors train their supervisees to use a structured format for case presentation during individual and group supervision sessions. We provide a basic framework in Handout 2.1 that includes five stages, with the first stage requiring the trainee to identify goals/objectives for case consultation with the supervisor or group. The format is intended to encourage active preparation and participation in supervision, while also providing an explicit process for thinking about casework. In our university seminars, we encourage supervises to present the case information in 7 minutes or less so that most of the supervision time may be spent on addressing the trainee's objectives.

HANDOUT 2.1   Case Consultation Format

STAGE 1: Consultation Concerns/Questions: Identify areas and objectives for consultation with supervisor and/or peers.

STAGE 2: Client Characteristics: Identify the client and present information relevant to case analysis such as gender, grade/age, family status, medical, and/or mental health diagnoses.

STAGE 3: Current Stage in Case Conceptualization: Identify stage of case (e.g., referral concern, assessment, intervention planning)

STAGE 4: Referral Concern: Identify specific area(s) of concern or need in clear, observable terms; identify discrepancy from peers if possible.

STAGE 5: Assessment Data: Present data useful for analysis and consultation during supervision.

STAGE 6: Intervention Recommendations: Identify interventions that align to assessment data, including evidence-base and plan for outcome evaluation.

Referral Concern

A well-developed referral concern helps to set the stage for a sound evaluation and informs the school psychologist about the reason for testing. Most often, teachers and parents refer a student for case study evaluation when they have concerns about the child's ability to benefit from his or her education or suspect an educational disability. Other reasons for referral may include student consideration for special programming, such as gifted and talented education, or vocational planning. Regardless of the source or content of the referral, school psychologists should understand both the purpose (how information will be used) and scope (details about the presenting concerns and how they impact the student's school performance) of the referral driving the evaluation. School psychologists are most commonly involved in evaluations when specific domains of functioning (i.e., intellectual, academic, linguistic, social/emotional) are in question and should gather as much information about how the child *currently* functions in these domains at the onset of the case study.

When evaluation is for the purpose of special education eligibility, information about the referral may first be explored in the domain meeting for the student. Domain meetings provide the school team and caregivers an opportunity to review and document the child's current functioning and also to identify specific domains of functioning (e.g., academic, intellectual, communication) for evaluation. School psychologists should be actively involved in the identification of specific referral questions and concerns during the domain meeting in order to meaningfully guide the evaluation. For example, a teacher may provide a vague statement indicating concern about a student's performance in the classroom, such as "Jose struggles to keep up with the curriculum," leading the team to indicate "achievement testing" is needed as part of the evaluation. With a little inquiry, the school psychologist may learn from the teacher that Jose struggles in the area of reading and, in particular, she has concerns about his reading comprehension. The school psychologist also noticed that Jose's state and district test scores reflect average to above average achievement in all academic areas except reading. The school psychologist may recommend changing the request for "achievement testing" to more specifically reflect the need for assessment in reading skills and achievement. This type of dialogue during the domain meeting leads to a clearer picture of the purpose and scope of the evaluation. It also protects client welfare by ensuring that unnecessary testing is not conducted.

Activity to support trainee development of referral concern

Supervisors can teach trainees to ask their referral sources many questions in their quest to formulate the referral concern. The following questions may help to guide discussions with relevant referral sources: (a) How long have you had these concerns? (b) How does the student perform in comparison to peers? (c) How frequently have you observed the problems? (d) What are examples of the problem? and (e) What information do you hope to learn from the evaluation? Trainees should then be encouraged to use this information to write specific referral questions (e.g., What is the student's level of cognitive development?) that will help to guide their evaluation of the child. A well-developed referral question will help to prevent the trainee from falling into the "assessment protocol" trap, where they choose evaluation tools that are commonly used for specific disability categories. Handout 2.2 is also an instructional tool that supervisors can use to help develop supervisee skills in case conceptualization and follows the "I do, we do, you do" format discussed in Chapter 1.

Assessment

As illustrated in Figure 2.1, a well-developed referral concern should be linked to targeted assessment that will help to answer questions about how a student functions in a given school setting. Because of the diagnostic (eligibility) responsibility involved with special education evaluations, school psychologists who supervise practicum candidates must ensure that the assessment practice of their trainees is sound by thoroughly monitoring the administration, scoring, and interpretation of assessment results. Given the vast number of assessment tools that school psychologists use in a school setting, it is unrealistic to expect the practicum candidate to be well trained in all. Harvey and Struzziero (2008) recommend that supervisors develop a model of assessment supervision that applies to multiple instruments and activities to address this issue and encourage supervisees to use their own methods for self-guided learning of new assessment tools. We recommend a variety of strategies for these purposes and suggest there are three main steps in supporting candidate assessment that can be characterized as: (a) developing the assessment plan, (b) monitoring administration of testing and data collection, and (c) supporting interpretation of assessment results.

Development of assessment plan

The National Association of School Psychologists' (NASP) (2000) *Professional Conduct Manual* suggests that psychological assessments are sound when they are multifaceted (multiple methods), comprehensive (cover all areas of the child's disability), fair (nonbiased), valid (ensure standardization), and useful (linked to referral, shared through a report, and lead to interventions). Most importantly, school psychologists should gather assessment information from multiple sources (e.g., parents, teachers, student) using multiple methods (e.g., record review, interview, observation, testing) in any

HANDOUT 2.2   Referral Concern Activity

Think of a referral concern that has been identified or discussed at your site. Use the table to identify the concern, transform it into a question, and identify the different assessment approaches that would answer the question.

Concern	Question	Sources of Information	Tools or Methods
I Do Example: The student isn't reading very well.	Does the student have the reading skills needed to make adequate progress in the assigned reading curriculum? Does the student need specialized instruction to make adequate progress in the third grade reading curriculum? Does the student meet the eligibility criteria for a Specific Learning Disability (SLD) as defined by state?	Academic measures to document student's skill in five areas of reading. Normative information to compare performance to expectations and calculate magnitude of discrepancy. Knowledge of expectations in classroom, instruction and skill to understand impact of discrepancy Information on history of difficulties and persistence Information on student's approach to reading	Summative evaluation: ■ Standardized reading measures ■ Reading fluency measures Formative evaluation: ■ Diagnostic reading inventories ■ Performance assessment ■ Permanent product Curriculum scope and sequence Teacher interview on history of difficulty, interventions used, and expectations for progress and growth Parent and student perspective of difficulties School records, including attendance Developmental or academic history
We Do Example: The student can't sit still in reading.			
You Do Example:			

29

given domain (e.g., intellectual, academic, communication) that is under evaluation. While it is critical that the student evaluation is comprehensive, it is both inefficient and unethical to conduct assessment that is unnecessary and/or does not lead to good decision making for the student (Sandoval & Irvin, 1990). School psychologists should be careful not to fall in the trap of simply using a common battery of assessments for specific types of referral concerns (e.g., specific learning disability, other health impairment) that occur frequently in school settings.

Supervision activity to support trainee development of assessment plan

Supervisors can encourage their supervisees to be actively involved in assessment planning by having trainees draft an initial assessment plan for evaluation in lieu of telling them which assessments to gather and administer. The Assessment Plan Worksheet in Handout 2.3 is a tool that can be used with supervisees and assist in helping them learn to link well-developed referral questions to a thoughtful assessment plan that will help to answer important questions about a student. It can also be used as a communication tool between the practicum candidate and the site and university supervisors during evaluation planning.

Test administration and data collection

Supervisors can expect that practicum candidates in school psychology will enter the field site with some training in the administration, scoring, and interpretation of standardized instruments and basic report writing. The depth and breadth of this training, however, may vary based on the home training institution. Alfonso, LaRocca, Oakland, and Spankos (2000) found that students typically submitted five to six scored protocols, wrote three to four reports, and took a competency exam in assessment courses. Candidate knowledge of various tools may also be limited, as training programs teach what they know, prefer, and have access to as resources. Some training programs may also prefer to focus on the use of less traditional tools such as curriculum-based measurement (CBM) and other authentic academic measures as part of an assessment series. It is important to understand how the scope and sequence of a particular candidate's training in assessment relates to his or her overall preparation for evaluation work during practicum. Multisource and multimethod assessment also requires practitioners to look beyond their test kits. It is, therefore, important to mentor trainees to use a variety of methods (record review, interview, observation, and testing) and gather information from a variety of sources (parents, teachers, and students) for an evaluation.

HANDOUT 2.3   Assessment Plan Worksheet

Referral Question	Assessment Tools	Source
Example. What is Alvin's level of social and emotional functioning?	Behavioral Assessment System for Children Interview Classroom Observations Office Discipline Referrals	Parent, teacher, student Parent, teacher, student Student observation

Supervision activities to support test administration and data collection

We recommend that supervisors develop specific strategies to support trainees in four main assessment methods: (a) review of records, (b) interviewing, (c) observations, and (d) testing. Novice trainees may become easily overwhelmed by the amount of information in student cumulative and special education records. Supervisors can teach supervisees to focus on the most salient information by using a structured record review template. Such a template can help to organize district test scores, relevant background information, important diagnostic information, and current interventions. An example template for this activity is included in Handout 2.4.

Several supervision activities are helpful in supporting trainee development in clinical interviewing. Trainees first need to understand what types of questions and content to obtain when interviewing students, parents, and teachers. It may be helpful to have supervisees use highly structured interview formats (e.g., Reich, Welner, & Herjanic, 1997) during initial interviews and move to semistructured and unstructured interviews as they gain comfort and proficiency with different informants. Before trainees conduct their first interview, supervisors may also take some time to role-play an interview session with the supervisee as practice to ensure familiarity and understanding of the interview questions. We have used this strategy in university-based settings and find that it is incredibly useful in helping the supervisee become more fluent with the interview questions and objectives. Trainees may need a few trial runs to "shake off the nerves," so to speak!

Supervisors may also consider observing trainees conduct their first few interviews so that they can provide explicit feedback about "soft" clinical skills such as the trainees' ability to build and maintain rapport, effectively use encouragers, and overall sensitivity toward the topic and client. In the absence of a live observation, supervisors can also have a supervisee either audio or video record client interviews so that they can analyze them together at a more convenient time. This type of activity might be most useful for a university-based supervisor who does not regularly observe trainees in the field activities. Having the trainee transcribe the recording is also a useful exercise by having them self-assess their own performance.

Classroom observations complement an evaluation by providing incredibly rich information about how a student interacts in his or her educational environment. Practicum supervisors should have their trainees spend a significant amount of time in observation activities early in the field experience. We recommend that supervisors assign supervisees a range of observations (classroom, student, data recording, and anecdotal) in the first few weeks. Box 2.1 includes a list of observations to consider.

HANDOUT 2.4   File Review Template

STUDENT IDENTIFYING INFORMATION:

Name:	DOB:
Current Grade:	Teachers:
Parent(s):	Phone #:
Date of Review:	

REFERRAL QUESTION OR CONCERN:

BIRTH AND DEVELOPMENTAL HISTORY:

MEDICAL OR TREATMENT HISTORY:
  Vision/Hearing:
  Other:

FAMILY OR SOCIAL HISTORY:

SCHOOL HISTORY:

Year	Grade	School	Attendance Rate

HISTORY OF SPECIAL EDUATION ELIGIBILITY:
What is this student's current eligibility:
Date/Grade of initial eligibility:
Dates/Grade of Re-evaluation:

Current services:

Service	Type (Direct or Consult)	Number of Minutes	Notes
Speech & Language			
Occupational Therapy			
Physical Therapy			
Nursing Services			
Psychological Services			
Other:			

(continued)

HANDOUT 2.4   File Review Template (*continued*)

BEHAVIORAL HISTORY/DISCIPLINE ISSUES:

Grade	Classroom Discipline	Office Referrals	Suspension	Support Programs

ASSESSMENTS:

State Assessments:

State Achievement Test Results: Scaled Score and Performance Level				
Grade	Reading	Writing	Math	Science
K				
1				
2				
3				

Curriculum Based Measurement (CBM):

Other District Assessments:

Current Performance Information: Review Progress Reports:

Class/Subject Area(s)	Grades				Teacher Comment(s)
	Q1	Q2	Q3	Q4	

INTERVENTIONS NOTED IN THE RECORD (INCLUDING PASS PLANS):

1. *GRADE:*

Intervention:

Supports/strategies:

Problem-solving completed date:

2. *GRADE:*

Intervention:

Supports/strategies:

Problem-solving completed date:

3. *GRADE:*

Intervention:

Supports/strategies:

Problem-solving completed date:

To extend this activity further, supervisors can direct supervisees to summarize each observation in a written summary. This offers the trainee practice in capturing the critical details from the observation, describing their observations using behavioral terms, and summarizing the information in a written document. It provides the supervisor information about both the trainee's skill in observation and written communication and helps to plan ahead for the report-writing process. An excellent way to ensure trainee accuracy in using various observation tools or methods is to schedule a few key observations where the supervisor and trainee can both observe simultaneously and determine the interobserver agreement. Box 2.2 provides a common method for calculating interobserver agreement. Supervisors and supervisees should strive for 80% or better agreement during observations. For trainees who may require additional practice with observations, it may also be practical and efficient to have them practice a variety of observation methods using very short video clips of different behaviors and classroom settings via an easily accessible website such as *YouTube*. Trainees can practice these skills outside of their time in the practicum setting to gain fluency with specific tools. Supervisors are then able to review the trainee's accuracy with the observations in a way similar to an activity where both supervisor and supervisee conduct a live observation together.

Testing for the purpose of special education eligibility is a high-stakes activity and supervisors should be thoughtful in their support of trainee development in this area. First, to ensure accuracy in test administration,

---

BOX 2.1   Suggested List of Practice Observations

General Education Classroom Observation
Special Education Classroom Observation
Unstructured Setting Observation (e.g., Lunch, Recess)
Student Observation #1: Anecdotal
Student Observation #2: Time On-Task
Student Observation #3: Antecedent Behavior Consequence (ABC)

BOX 2.2   Calculating Interobserver Agreement

Method: Point-by-Point Agreement Ratio assesses whether there is agreement on each instance of an observed behavior. This method is used most often with interval recording, such as a time-on-task instrument. Interobserver agreement is calculated using the following formula:
A = number of agreements for each interval observed
D = number of disagreements for each interval observed
Agreement = $[A/(A + D)] \times 100$

supervisors should observe trainees conducting assessments with their first few cases. If a trainee is using a new test or assessment procedure, some additional instruction might be necessary, such as using assigned readings, attending a workshop, providing simulated activities, or having the supervisee observe the supervisor or other school psychologist administer, score, and interpret the data. Some of the supervisors we have worked with also report that it is quite effective to role-play the part of the student during a trainee's practice administration. Once accuracy in administration has been established, the supervisor can feel more comfortable providing the trainee additional independence conducting assessment with students. At this stage, supervisors and supervisees may find it helpful to collaborate on a few case studies, with each completing assessment for various portions of the evaluation and coming together to analyze and interpret the data. A final move to independence with assessments would allow the supervisee independence in scheduling and conducting assessments for casework on his or her own while keeping the supervisor up-to-date on case developments through weekly supervision meetings.

Interpretation of assessment results

Supervisors should assist their trainees in understanding the link between assessment and intervention. Assessment should be comprehensive enough so that school psychologists can draw conclusions or interpretations from the data in the final stages of an evaluation. These interpretations will lead directly to intervention recommendations and educational planning. Practitioners draw conclusions or make interpretations from the data by looking for consistencies in the evaluation findings. For example, a practitioner may note that a classroom observation, teacher interview, and parent rating scale all indicate that a student has difficulty with social skills. Defensible interpretations should always be supported by more than one piece of data.

Supervision activity to support trainee interpretations of assessment results

Making sense of the data is perhaps one of the most demanding jobs for the novice practicum student, as it requires clinical judgment for each unique student and case. Trainees cannot follow a written protocol or standardized procedure to make interpretations about factors that impact student performance. Instead, they need to learn to develop sound hypotheses that help to explain poor student performance in a given area of functioning. These hypotheses should be tied clearly to data that confirm or refute them. Supervisors can help trainees improve their clinical judgment by providing an explicit framework for evaluating their hypotheses (interpretations) with the data they have collected through case study evaluation. Using a visual or graphic organizer may

TABLE 2.1 Sample Data Guide					
Interpretation	Record Review	Interview	Observation	Tests	How Many Pieces of Data?

help the novice practicum candidate learn to apply this logic in the early stages of casework. An example is provided in Table 2.1. Supervisors can ask their trainees to use this table to present their interpretations as an exercise during individual supervision sessions. As the trainee gains fluency with this skill, the use of such an explicit framework may be slowly removed or modified.

Intervention

Assessments used for special education evaluation should provide information that is reliable and valid for making decisions about eligibility and determining student need (Individuals with Disabilities Education Act, 2004). School psychologists help school teams translate evaluation information into practice by assisting with the identification of evidence-based interventions and the collection of student outcome data. This is most often accomplished via recommendations that are provided at the end of an evaluation report for the student. At the foundation of evidence-based interventions is a clear link between referral, assessment, and intervention. Not only must today's school psychologist be able to design student interventions that are empirically supported, they must also be able to monitor both treatment integrity (i.e., degree to which an intervention is implemented as designed) and student outcomes (e.g., response to intervention). These last two components, while critical, are often overlooked in school-based intervention designs.

Supervision activity to support intervention

Supervisors can assist practicum candidates in their intervention work by training them to engage in evidence-based practice, which is twofold. First, supervisees need to learn how to select and use empirically validated interventions, requiring them to be critical consumers of research. This task can be daunting given the high volume of commercial interventions and web-based resources that are available and marketed as "evidence-based." An excellent resource to share and use with trainees is the guide published by the U.S. Department of Education (2003) for identifying and implementing evidence-based interventions. It offers a step-by-step approach for

TABLE 2.2 Summary of Outcome Data				
Treatment Goal	**Treatment Integrity**	**Trendline Analysis**	**Effect Size**	**Decision**
Met	90%	Positive	Percent Non-Overlapping Data (PND) = 96%	Effective Intervention

determining the quality of research supporting an intervention. It may also be helpful for supervisees to keep a log or running list of evidence-based interventions they identified over the course of the practicum training and later catalogue them for their own reference. This is a great way to encourage trainees' investment in their own professional development and begin to organize resources they may use in later practice settings.

The second component of evidence-based practice that is critical for trainees to develop is their ability to evaluate their own practice. That is, they need to determine whether the student interventions they implement do what they predict and expect. We suggest that supervisors train practicum candidates to embed the following three components into intervention designs from the onset: (a) a measure of treatment fidelity, (b) measure(s) of student outcome, and (c) a guide for making data-based decisions. A student's response to an intervention should not be evaluated in the absence of information about treatment integrity. If an intervention is implemented with low levels of integrity, the "outcome data" is essentially a reflection of the student's performance under the status quo (no intervention). Finally, trainees should know in advance of making decisions about the data how they will analyze the information (e.g., visual analysis, effect size). The novice trainee may easily become overwhelmed in making sense of all of the information. We recommend using a graphic or visual organizer to help the trainee summarize the data. An example is provided in Table 2.2

CASE CONCEPTUATIONAL IN CONSULTATION

With a projected shortage of school psychologists through 2020 (Curtis, Chesno Grier, & Hunley, 2004), emphasis has been placed on reducing the time school psychologists spend on traditional special education evaluations to focus more on roles that are linked directly to interventions within the context of a multitiered, public health approach to service delivery (Castillo et al., 2012; Curtis et al. 2004; Dawson et al., 2004). Such a shift requires using consultation and collaborative problem solving with other adults (e.g., parents, teachers, other school personnel) who work directly with students in school, home, and community settings. School psychologists currently dedicate approximately 20% of their time to consultation activities (Castillo et al., 2012; Fagan & Wise, 2007), with the majority (96% or more) engaging in student-focused consultation (Castillo et al., 2012).

While consultation remains a significant role of the school psychologist, there is emerging concern about the preparation and training of school psychologists as consultants. Both the lack of in-depth training within specific models (Anton-LaHart & Rosenfield, 2004) and the lack of direct supervision and feedback (Anton-LaHart & Rosenfield, 2004; Newell, 2012) have been documented. Some common concerns that arise for consultants-in-training (CIT's) fall in the following topical areas: (a) general knowledge of the problem-solving process, (b) competence in the problem-solving stages, (c) using data, (d) communication skills, (e) relationships, (f) consultative role, (g) student status, and (h) supervision (Newman, 2012). Thus, providing direct supervision in the use of a structured consultation model with ample opportunity for feedback may be particularly helpful for the novice practicum candidate.

Practicum supervisors should help trainees first understand first what is meant by consultation in the schools. Candidates may easily mistake much of what they do (e.g., quick recommendations, teacher follow-up, classroom support) as consultation without a clear understanding of their role as a school-based consultant. Consultation is best characterized as an indirect helping approach whereby a consultant helps clients (i.e., students) through direct interactions with consultees (e.g., teachers, parents, other school personnel; Erchul & Sheridan, 2014). The goals of consultation are to both improve client outcomes and increase the consultee's skill or capacity to handle similar situations in the future. While there are a variety of approaches used in education (e.g., instructional, mental health, behavioral, conjoint behavioral), a problem-solving or behavioral approach to consultation is relatively popular in school settings. This is most likely attributed to the structured interview procedures of behavioral consultation and use of applied behavior-analytic techniques (Erchul & Sheridan, 2014), as well as its use in multitiered systems of support.

School-based behavioral consultation is conceptualized as a five-stage process (Kratochwill, Elliott, & Rotto, 1995) that includes: (a) relationship building, (b) problem identification, (c) problem analysis, (d) intervention implementation, and (e) program evaluation.

While supervisors should consider how to support trainee development in each stage of the model, individual trainees may require additional support with specific consultation factors or skills. It has been suggested that relationship quality, treatment acceptability, and treatment integrity are key factors related to consultation outcomes (Frank & Kratochwill, 2012). We, therefore, pay particular attention to these areas in our discussion related to supervision activities in the following section.

Supervision Activities for Case Conceptualization in Consultation

Training in consultation is multilayered and complex and an extensive discussion of supervision issues in consultation is beyond the scope of this book. Instead, we recommend that school psychologists supervising novice candidates focus on foundational consultation skills and process knowledge during the practicum training. Remember that the novice candidate will be largely concerned with skill acquisition during early training experiences. As such, we suggest that supervisors focus first on addressing trainee knowledge of the processes and procedures of a particular consultation model. Supervisors can support trainee development in the use of a structured consultation model by helping to orient practicum candidates to resources that will assist in their practice. Because our discussion has focused heavily on the use of school-based problem-solving consultation, we recommend *Behavioral Consultation in Applied Settings: An Individual Guide* (Bergan & Kratochwill, 1990) and *Conjoint Behavioral Consultation: Promoting Family School Connections and Interventions, Second Edition* (Sheridan & Kratochwill, 2007). Both books provide procedural guides to the implementation of specific behavioral consultation models, including interview guides and objective-based checklists. The books are excellent resources for a university-based consultation course or as part of a recommended reading list for trainees.

Supervisors can provide practice with a specific model by facilitating opportunity to engage in consultation with a teacher and/or parent in the school setting and closely supervise the experience. Close supervision could include regular case consultation, observation of consultation sessions, video or audio analysis of interviews, and review of trainee process notes and consultation logs. We have found it particularly helpful to have trainees use the consultation checklists provided in the Bergan and Kratochwill (1990) book that correspond to each interview to conduct self- and peer-assessment of consultation activities as part of a course in consultation or a practicum seminar. Viewing select interviews or portions of sessions in class as part of a group supervision activity is also an excellent way for trainees to receive peer and supervisor feedback. This type of activity could also be easily facilitated in a field setting in either individual or group formats.

As noted previously, particular attention to trainee activities in addressing both treatment acceptability and integrity may help to promote positive client and consultee outcomes. As indirect service providers, consultants must rely on teachers and parents to deliver interventions and monitor student progress. Novice candidates are often unprepared for the challenges associated with treatment fidelity and are frequently disappointed when implementation efforts fall short of their expectations. Supervisors should help to prepare candidates for these challenges by both normalizing the experience and helping them to use strategies to promote and monitor integrity. We feel that it is incredibly important in the early stages of consultation training that candidates understand their role as it relates to the promotion and measurement of treatment integrity. Supervisees can easily lose motivation and take on a "blaming" attitude where they attribute failed interventions only to consultee-related characteristics (e.g., lack of skill or motivation). Supervisors can encourage trainees to hold realistic perceptions of their work by talking about these challenges early in the training experience and helping trainees understand that they are an integral component of the consultation process.

Teachers and parents are more likely to deliver interventions with integrity when they are perceived as acceptable for use. In other words, consumers who are happy with a product will use it! Supervisors should encourage trainees to promote acceptability by designing interventions that are aligned to student needs, feasible to implement, and considered effective. As part of treatment planning, supervisors can also encourage trainees to use an instrument such as the Intervention Rating Profile—15 (IRP; Witt & Elliott, 1985) or the Treatment Evaluation Inventory (TEI; Kazdin, 1980) to verify and measure treatment acceptability with parents and teachers. Supervisees can then address any issues of acceptability or implementation challenges during the planning stages and before treatment begins.

Supervisors should also encourage trainees to incorporate strategies to promote and evaluate treatment integrity as part of a comprehensive intervention plan. Based on a review of current research, Frank and Kratochwill (2012) suggested the following strategies to promote integrity: (a) make use of treatment scripts; (b) implement consultee goal-setting and feedback procedures; (c) incorporate performance feedback interviews; (d) directly train teachers on treatment integrity for each intervention; and (e) make use of interventions that have high treatment acceptability for the teachers. Supervisors can also train candidates to design a measure of integrity by creating a simple checklist of intervention steps that can be used to monitor implementation efforts. Treatment integrity can be calculated by dividing the number of treatment components (steps) by the total number of components in the intervention and multiply by 100. This information should be considered during the implementation stage to determine if more consultee support is needed (e.g., additional training, treatment modifications) and also during any final evaluation of student outcomes.

Practicum candidates will also require support while learning how to build collaborative relationships during their early work as consultants. Remember, their ability to influence and work with others is critical to their effectiveness at improving outcomes for parents, teachers, and students. Sheridan and Kratochwill (2007) recognize four skill domains that require attention: communication, perspective taking, building partnerships, and managing conflict. While a detailed discussion of strategies in each of these areas is beyond the scope of this book, we have incorporated skills in these domains as part of a checklist for monitoring student consultation performance. The checklist in Appendix C can be used as both an instructional and evaluation tool for assisting in supervision of consultation work. It is designed for use in the supervision of a behavioral consultation model.

CASE CONCEPTULATION IN COUNSELING

Counseling is a relatively small part of the contemporary school psychologist's role. In the most recent national survey of the field, school psychologists reported dedicating an average of 5.8% of their time in individual student counseling and 3.1% of their time to conducting student groups (Castillo et al., 2012). In fact, nearly one third reported engaging in no counseling during the 2009–2012 school years, a figure that is double that of 20 years ago. In addition, a recent survey of practicum students (Tarquin & Truscott, 2006) revealed that assessment tended to be the primary focus of their fieldwork with relatively little emphasis on counseling or consultation. Despite efforts to broaden the role of the school psychologist, many training programs also still emphasize assessment-related activities as part of their training model.

What this suggests is that school psychologists supervising candidates may lack both personal training and opportunity to facilitate activities related to counseling and may supervise trainees that have little to no training in counseling by the time they begin the practicum. We have raised these concerns not to suggest that counseling is an unimportant role for the school psychologist, but rather because there are some very real challenges and limitations to the current training of school psychologists in this domain of practice. We thus strongly advocate that school psychologists supervising practicum candidates carefully consider their own training and experience in counseling, candidate training, and relevant site characteristics (e.g., opportunity for closely supervised counseling experience) when facilitating counseling-related activities.

Counseling refers to activities where the school psychologist provides direct interventions to a student or a group of students and may include services such as crisis intervention, psychoeducational counseling or individual counseling (Reschly & Wilson, 1995). Most often, school psychologists provide counseling services to meet service requirements as part of student Individualized Education Plans (IEPs). As such, school-based counseling services are closely tied to student school performance and largely focus on student behavioral and social issues in the education setting.

Supervision Activities for Case Conceptualization in Counseling

First and foremost, supervisors should carefully select counseling cases for practicum candidates by identifying students who have relatively mild social, behavioral, or emotional difficulties. That is, supervisors should assign the easiest cases to trainees and refer students who have more significant and persistent mental health concerns to seasoned school-based mental health practitioners or outside service providers. That said, there are a range of mild student issues that may be an excellent fit for individual or group counseling activities, including students who need support paying attention, maintaining organization, developing and maintaining relationships with peers, and improving emotional regulation (commonly referred to as anger management), to name a few.

Before any case assignment, supervisors should facilitate opportunities for trainees to observe others (i.e., primary supervisor, other school-based mental health providers) in counseling activities. Supervisors may be able to best achieve this by cocounseling with candidates in individual and group settings and sharing casework. After an initial period of observation (e.g., 2–3 weeks), the trainee should be encouraged to participate more actively during counseling sessions. Supervisors can do this by assigning small roles (e.g., lead an activity, facilitate a topical discussion) and taking time in both pre- and post session supervision to prepare the candidate and provide feedback on performance. By the end of the counseling experience, the candidate may be ready to lead one or two sessions independently with careful pre- and post supervision.

In the initial stages of case assignment, supervisors should carefully review and support activities related to obtaining informed consent and assent for services and explaining the limits of confidentiality to students and parents, two ethical issues central to direct intervention work with students. It is useful to have a general consent form that can be easily modified for individual and group counseling work available to students at the site—an example is provided in Handout 2.5. Informed consent should be provided in writing before services begin and include the following elements: (a) reason for counseling services, (b) goals of counseling, (c) frequency and duration of services, (d) formats and methods, (e) anticipated benefits, (f) possible risks, and (g) alternatives to services offered (Plotts & Lasser, 2013).

Supervisors should also help trainees in developing treatment plans that are clearly aligned to student needs and emphasize the monitoring of student outcomes. Counseling services should be designed to meet specific, measurable goals, and objectives, which are often aligned to student IEP goals. Goals should identify the *learner,* the *target behavior,* the *conditions,* and the *criteria for acceptable performance.* Some example goals are

Dear Parent,

I am a school psychology practicum student at **Fairbanks Elementary** who is training under the supervision of Mrs. Smith. I want to offer your child the opportunity to participate in a counseling group. The group will meet weekly during second period with four other children for a total of eight sessions and aim to improve social skills.

Because it is important for children to discuss things they do not want other adults to know about, the specific content of each counseling session is held confidential with some important exceptions. Because our first goal is to keep children safe, confidentiality will not be maintained if your child is deemed to pose a risk to himself or herself or to others, or if there is information that suggests a child is being abused. Another exception to confidentially is that I will discuss your child's counseling sessions with my supervisor. However, supervision will also be confidential in nature. A final exception is that I may discuss your child's sessions with my school-based supervisor but, again, such discussions will be held confidentially. Specific information will not be shared with other school-based personnel unless safety issues are present that require action at the school level.

The proposed child counseling sessions will not be held unless your child also agrees to participate. I will fully explain the rules regarding confidentiality to him or her so that he or she can make an informed decision. Children also have the right to terminate counseling at any time without being required to justify this decision. There will be no negative consequences for your child if he or she decides to terminate counseling.

Sincerely,

_____

Practicum Student's Name/Phone Number   Signature of Practicum Student

_____

☐ I consent to let my child receive counseling services

☐ I <u>do not</u> consent to allow my child to receive counseling services

Parent's signature: _____
                              (Signature)   Phone Number/E-mail

Child's name: _____   Date: _____

> **BOX 2.3   Example Counseling Goals**
>
> **Referral Concern: Social Skills/Interactions**
> Susan will use at least two different greetings when entering the classroom in the morning to greet her teacher and peers by April, 2015.
>
> **Referral Concern: Emotion Regulation/Aggression**
> Juan will identify three coping strategies he can use when he feels angry in response to peer conflicts by December, 2015.
>
> **Referral Concern: Executive Functioning/Organization**
> Devon will submit homework 90% of the time in math class for 3 consecutive weeks by January, 2015.

included in Box 2.3. We have also developed a basic process for providing referral-driven and goal-oriented evidence-based counseling support in the school setting (see Handout 2.6). Supervisors can use this resource to help trainees conceptualize their case and monitor trainee activities over the course of the counseling experience. It may also serve as a good resource for case consultation in individual or group supervision.

Trainees will likely need a lot of support figuring out exactly what to do during individual or group counseling sessions. Novice practicum candidates will benefit from using scripted or highly structured models of intervention (e.g., treatment manuals). Supervisors can assist trainees by orienting them to evidence-based resources that are well suited to school-based counseling. *Cognitive behavior therapy* (CBT; Kendall & Hedtke, 2006) is both an effective and popular treatment that can be used to address a variety of student issues such as emotional regulation, relaxation, social skills, anxiety, communication, and problem solving. *Solution-focused* models are also a particularly good fit for the school setting, as they are designed to offer brief and targeted counseling for students, which is well-suited to school schedules and time constraints (e.g., weekly 30-minute sessions). The *Brief Counseling That Works: A Solution-Focused Therapy Approach for School Counselors and Other Mental Health Professionals* (Sklare, 2014) is an excellent resource for beginning counselors. Finally, NASP's publication entitled *School Psychologist as Counselor* (Plotts & Lasser, 2013) is specifically targeted to the field and offers information about a variety of counseling orientations.

The final role supervisors can play in supporting practicum candidate development in counseling is to train them to evaluate and document student outcomes. A useful method for record keeping is SOAP notes—subjective, objective, assessment, and plan (Cameron & Turtle-Song, 2002; Weed, 1971). The first two components of a SOAP note (subjective and objective) correspond to data collection. The subjective note should reflect

HANDOUT 2.6   Treatment Plan Development

Step 1: Identify Referral Process and Concerns: How did you find your case? Was it referred through a team, teacher, or parent? What are the presenting concerns?

Step 2: Identify Treatment Goals: What do you want the student(s) to do by the end of the counseling experience? What are the criteria for success, including timelines and desired outcomes?

Step 3: Identify Therapeutic Theory or Approach: What orientation will guide your practice and is best matched to the student needs? Is there a curriculum or resource you will use? Is the approach considered effective?

Step 4: Provide Overview of Session Objectives, Content, and Timelines: What is your plan for each counseling session? How many sessions will you need with the student(s)?

Step 5: Identify Evaluation and Documentation Systems: How do you know it's working? How will you monitor treatment outcomes? How will you keep records of the counseling process and outcomes?

Step 6: Termination Plan: When and how will you end your sessions? What follow-up actions or activities are required for maintenance or further treatment?

BOX 2.4 SOAP Note Example for School-Based Counseling Case

This is a SOAP note documented for the fifth session with a 10-year-old girl who has difficulty maintaining attention in the classroom.

9/2/20XX; 2 p.m. (S) Reports she likes counseling and feels that it has been helpful (high motivation to continue); feels like she is able to pay attention better in class; teacher reports her work completion has improved and she needs to redirect her less often to stay on task. (O) Highly engaged during sessions; participated in all activities with positive affect and persistence; came to session highly disorganized (e.g., messy backpack, school work in wrong folders). (A) Attention and organizational difficulties/consider other executive functioning areas of impairment. (P) Next session: 9/9/20XX; modify self-monitoring form for math class; assess using organizational checklist. N. Smith, Practicum Student (signature).

---

the client's perceptions of the problem (e.g., client's thoughts and feelings; what others tell you about the client), while the objective note should be factual (e.g., quantifiable). The assessment (A) note should include a practitioner's *clinical impressions* of the client's difficulties. Because the SOAP note method originates from a medical model, this section often includes a diagnosis (e.g., attention deficit/hyperactivity disorder), but we feel that this can easily be adapted to school-based nomenclature (e.g., attention difficulties). The last section of the note is the plan (P), which consists of both an action plan (treatment direction) and client prognosis (expected growth). Box 2.4 provides an example of SOAP notes for a school-based counseling case.

EVALUATION OF THE SUPERVISEE

In this early stage of the practicum, supervisors should make it a habit to review the supervisee's training plan and ensure that activities and goals are being addressed. Regular monitoring of the plan will help prevent or proactively address potential conflicts among the university, the field site, and trainee expectations. Supervisors should consider incorporating a monthly review of the plan during individual supervision to ensure that the training is progressing as planned and determine if modification should be considered.

A formal site visit from the university supervisor may also be beneficial in these early stages of the practicum. The purpose of this site visit is to establish regular communication between the site and university supervisor, discuss expectations for training, and review important processes and procedures, such as formal evaluation, assignments, and supervision formats. It is important for the supervisee to be present during this meeting and take an active role in the discussion about his or her training and professional development. Site supervisors should take time to review the unique

Student: Supervisor:

School/District: Date:

Requirements

Assignment Checklist:
- ☐ Practicum Proposal
- ☐ Functional Behavior Assessment/Behavior Intervention Plan (FBA/BIP)
- ☐ Psychoeducational Evaluation #1
- ☐ Intervention Project
- ☐ Activities Checklist
- ☐ Hours Log
- ☐ Supervisor Evaluation

Things to Discuss

- ✓ Supervision
- ✓ Student Progress
- ✓ Questions Regarding Use of Training Database or Supervision Expectations
- ✓ Assess That Support From University Is Adequate
- ✓ Supervisor and/or Student Questions

Additional Notes:

characteristics of the site and discuss opportunities and experiences that are available to the student. University supervisors should ensure that all training expectations and requirements will be met and also assess whether the current university support for training is appropriate for the trainee's needs in the site. Both field and university supervisors should keep a written record of what is discussed during this visit. A sample form that can be used to both structure and document the visit is included in Handout 2.7. These notes can be filed with the trainee's training records for the year and also used for reference in subsequent visits and supervision sessions.

SUPERVISOR TO-DO LIST

- ☐ Introduce case conceptualization expectations and format
- ☐ Train supervisee to link referral, assessment, and intervention
- ☐ Plan for trainee consultation with parents and teachers
- ☐ Assess trainee readiness and opportunity for counseling activities
- ☐ Monitor supervisee training plan and goals
- ☐ Conduct site and university visit to review expectations and establish regular communication

REFERENCES

Alfonso, V. C., LaRocca, R., Oakland, T. D., & Spankos, A. (2000). The course on individual cognitive assessment. *School Psychology Review, 29,* 52–64.

Anton-LaHart, J., & Rosenfield, S. (2004). A survey of preservice consultation training in school psychology programs. *Journal of Educational & Psychological Consultation, 15,* 41–62. doi:10.1207/s1532768xjepc1501_2.

Bergan, J. R., & Kratochwill, T. R. (1990). *Behavioral consultation in applied settings.* New York, NY: Plenum.

Cameron, S., & Turtle-Song, I. (2002). Learning to write case notes using the SOAP format. *Journal of Counseling and Development, 80,* 286–292.

Castillo, J. M., Curtis, M. J., & Gelley, C. (2012). School psychology 2010: School psychologists' professional practices and implications for the field—part 2. *NASP Communiqué, 40*(7), 1, 28–30.

Curtis, M. J., Chesno Grier, J. E., & Hunley, S. A. (2004). The changing face of school psychology: Trends in data and projects for the future. *School Psychology Review, 33*(1), 49–66.

Dawson, M., Cummings, J. A., Harrison, P. L., Short, R. J., Gorin, S., & Palomares, R. (2004). The 2002 multisite conference on the future of school psychology: Next steps. *School Psychology Review, 33,* 115–125.

Erchul, W. P., & Sheridan, S. M. (2014). The state of scientific research in school consultation. In W. P. Erchul & S. M. Sheridan (Eds.), *Handbook of research in school consultation,* (2nd ed.). New York, NY: Routledge.

Fagan, T. K., & Wise, P. S. (2007). *School psychology: Past, present, and future* (3rd ed.). Bethesda, MD: National Association of School Psychologists.

Frank, J. L., & Kratochwill, T. R. (2012). School-based problem solving consultation: Plotting a new course for evidence-based research and practice in consultation. In W. P. Erchul & S. M. Sheridan (Eds.), *Handbook of research in school consultation*, (2nd ed.). New York, NY: Routledge.

Harvey, V. S., & Struzziero, J. A. (2008). *Professional development and supervision of school psychologists: From intern to expert* (2nd ed.). Thousand Oaks, CA: Corwin Press and National Association of School Psychologists.

Individuals With Disabilities Education Improvement Act of 2004, Pub. L. No. 108–446, 118 Stat. 2647 (2004).

Kazdin, A. E. (1980). Acceptability of alternative treatment for deviant child behavior. *Journal of Applied Behavior Analysis, 13,* 259–273.

Kendall, P. C., & Hedtke, K. (2006). *Cognitive-behavior therapy for anxious children: Therapist manual* (3rd ed.). Ardmore, PA: Workbook.

Kratochwill, T. R., Elliott, S. N., & Rotto, P. C. (1995). Best practices in school-based behavioral consultation. In A. Thomas & J. Grimes (Eds.), *Best practices in school psychology III* (pp. 519–535). Bethesda, MD: National Association of School Psychologists.

National Association of School Psychologist. (2000). *Professional conduct manual* (3rd ed.). Bethesda, MD: Author.

Newell, M. (2012). Transforming knowledge to skill: Evaluating the consultation competence of novice school-based consultants. *Consulting Psychology Journal: Practice and Research, 64,* 8–28. doi:10.1037/a0027741.

Newman, D. (2012). Supervision of school-based consultation training: Addressing the concerns of novice consultants. In S. Rosenfield (Ed.) *Becoming a school consultant: Lessons learned.* New York, NY: Routledge.

Plotts, C., & Lasser, J. (2013). *School psychology as counselor: A practitioner's handbook.* Bethesda, MD: National Association of School Psychologists.

Reich, W., Welner, Z., & Herjanic, B. (1997). *Diagnostic interview for children and adolescents—IV computer program.* North Tonawanda, NY: Multi-Health Systems.

Reschly, D. J., & Wilson, M. S. (1995). School psychology faculty and practitioners: 1986–1991 trends in demographic characteristics, roles, satisfaction, and system reform. *School Psychology Review, 24*(1), 62–80.

Sandoval, J., & Irvin, M. G. (1990). Legal and ethical issues in the assessment of children. In C. R. Reynolds & R. W. Kamphaus (Eds.), *Handbook of psychological and educational assessment of children: Intelligence and achievement.* New York, NY: Guilford Press.

Sheridan, S. M., & Kratochwill, T. R. (2007). Conjoint behavioral consultation: Promoting family-school connections and interventions (2nd ed.). New York, NY: Springer.

Sklare, G. B. (2014). Brief counseling that works: A solution-focused approach for school counselors and other mental health professionals (3rd ed.). Thousand Oaks, CA: Corwin Press.

Tarquin, K. M., & Truscott, S. D. (2006). School psychology student's perceptions of their practicum experiences. *Psychology in the Schools, 43*(6), 727–736.

United States Department of Education. (2003). Identifying and implementing educational practices supported by rigorous evidence: A user-friendly guide. Washington, DC: Author.

Weed, L. L. (1971). Quality control and the medical record. *Archive of Internal Medicine, 127,* 101–105.

Witt, J. C., & Elliott, S. N. (1985). Acceptability of classroom intervention strategies. In T. R. Kratochwill (Ed.), *Advances in school psychology* (Vol. 4, pp. 251–288). Mahwah, NJ: Erlbaum.

THREE

FOUNDATIONS OF SPECIAL EDUCATION

While school psychologists engage in any number of activities to support regular education, a primary focus is still special education and related services (Castillo, Curtis, & Gelley, 2012). As such, practicum trainees need to understand the link between case study evaluations and the provision of special education services. Many practicum candidates will likely have completed coursework in legal and ethical issues related to special education, as well as multiple assessment courses, before the practicum begins. Trainees must gain an understanding of special education services beyond eligibility activities, including meaningful goal development, placement, and interventions that align to student needs identified through evaluation. This chapter addresses supervision related to trainee knowledge and skills required for the provision of special education services in the schools, including eligibility determination and service delivery.

UNDERSTANDING THE SPECIAL EDUCATION PROCESS

To fulfill the mandate identified in the most recent reauthorization of the Individuals with Disabilities Education Improvement Act (IDEIA)—that is, that all students with, or suspected of having, disabilities are entitled to a *free and appropriate public education (FAPE)* in the *least restrictive environment (LRE)*—school districts are required to provide all students with (a) evaluation and identification; (b) an individualized education program (IEP) and related services; (c) placement; (d) funding; and (e) procedural safeguards (Bateman & Linden, 2012). Individual state governments turn federal guidelines into rules and regulations that are translated by individual school districts or local education agencies (LEAs) into policies and procedures. Supervisees must learn and start to understand the application of both the state and federal guidelines that describe service delivery, and their local school system's translation of the rules and regulations into effective programs. As a result, supervisors can design and facilitate activities that allow supervisees to understand the many legal and ethical issues that define professional practice.

Supervisees may best understand district procedures for compliance with federal and state special education rules and regulations by reviewing relevant district resources (e.g., special education procedure manuals) and participating in staff orientation and other relevant professional development. Supervisors should be careful to highlight how district procedures are aligned to state and federal guidelines and ensure compliance with these standards. In addition, supervisees should be orientated to district compliance officers and legal resources; the process for identification, evaluation, and service delivery; and the process for resolving a special education dispute in the district. Central to an understanding of the special education process in schools is recognition that it is not just a paperwork process; rather, the rules and regulations help teams understand how to design and provide individualized services.

Supervision Activities to Facilitate an Understanding of School District Procedures

A supervisor can make available all important, updated district procedures for special education identification and eligibility (knowing full well that this may be an overwhelming amount of information) and help to translate this information for supervisees. For example, supervisors may provide instruction with the following school procedures: (a) the student referral process, (b) evaluation assignment and procedures, (c) timelines and requirements for team activities, (d) the meaning and implementation of obtaining informed consent from parents, (e) requirements and practices for parent involvement, (f) summarizing results, (g) determining eligibility, and (h) IEP development and implementation. This could include providing the district procedural manual to review, visual aids such as flowcharts for procedures, a calendar that includes timelines for evaluations, or district professional development related to special education and/or compliance.

The IEP Team

As mandated by the IDEIA 2004, the identification of disabilities is a "team" decision. This "team" is unique to each student and further identified according to the student's needs, referral concern, and evaluation required. According to IDEIA 2004, Section 1414(d)(1)(B), the IEP team includes "(i) the parents of a child with a disability; (ii) not less than one regular education teacher of such child (if the child is, or may be, participating in the regular education environment; (iii) not less than one special education teacher, or where appropriate, not less than one special education provider of such child; (iv) a representative of the local educational agency; (v) an individual who can interpret the instructional implications of evaluation results; (vi) at the discretion of the parent or the agency, other individuals who have knowledge or special expertise regarding the child, including related services personnel as appropriate; and (vii) whenever appropriate, the child with a disability." The law does not require that a school psychologist, specifically, be present. However, school psychologists are key school personnel who often fill several important roles, namely acting as an individual who can interpret evaluation results, a related services personnel with special expertise, and even a representative of the local educational agency.

Perhaps the most prominent role of the school psychologist on the IEP team is to assist the team in interpreting evaluation results. This often includes assisting the team in clearly developing strong referral questions during the domain meeting, identifying appropriate assessment methods during evaluation, linking evaluation results to the 13 federal disability categories, and identifying appropriate interventions and district supports, as necessary. For a full discussion of case conceptualization activities related to determining special education eligibility, see Chapter 2. Supervisors should also orient trainees to the format and process for IEP meetings within the district. Supervisors may consider reviewing the following with the novice trainee: (a) the team member responsible for facilitating the meeting, (b) school personnel involved in the meeting and various roles, (c) the identified LEA representative responsible for allocating district resources, and (d) the general meeting format. In addition, supervisors should invite practicum candidates to a few meetings during the training and discuss the role of each attendee specifically as it relates to the requirements for IDEIA.

Summarizing and Presenting Results

Results from a case study evaluation are disseminated to the IEP team through both written and oral reports. The main consumers of these reports are the parents and teachers working most closely with the individual student. In addition, IEP meetings can be a very emotional experience for parents, students, and school personnel. As such, school psychologists need to deliver these reports in a format that is acceptable, easy to understand, and user friendly.

Summarizing results in writing

School psychologists need strong oral and written communication skills so that they can share important evaluation information with teachers, parents, and students. As outlined in Sattler (2001), the objectives of a psycho-educational report are the following: (a) provide accurate assessment information to referral sources; (b) provide clinical information about hypotheses, interventions, and program evaluation; (c) provide meaningful baseline data; and (d) to serve as a legal document. While there are some variations in report structure based on individual and district preferences (e.g., personal style) and type of report (e.g., academic, behavioral), it is beneficial to provide trainees with some common elements and/or outlines for report writing so that they can learn to streamline the process of sharing information and become proficient in the process. Many traditional reports include the following sections: (a) identifying information, (b) assessment instruments, (c) referral, (d) background, (e) observation during assessment, (f) assessment results and clinical impressions, (g) recommendations, (h) summary, and (i) signature (Sattler, 2001).

While a more traditional approach may feel very familiar, there is evidence that teachers prefer reports organized by theme versus a test-by-test format (Pelco, Ward, Coleman, & Young, 2009). Theme-based reports can be organized around areas of functioning (e.g., social/emotional, academic), hypotheses (e.g., the student's reading achievement is low due to problems with fluency, or referral questions (e.g., what are the student's reading skills and achievement?). Teachers prefer reports that focus on referral questions and educational recommendations because they identify a clear purpose (referral) for the evaluation and help them better inform their classroom instruction (recommendations). With an increased focus on the use of multitiered systems of support (MTSS) in school settings, practitioners may also find a *solution-focused* report format quite useful. Solution-focused reports largely use formative assessment data (i.e., progress monitoring data) versus the summative information that is presented in a more traditional report (Brown-Chidsey & Andren, 2013).

Above all, trainees need to understand how to write reports so that they are consumer friendly and meaningful for the teachers, parents, and students that read them. While the average reading grade level for current psycho-educational reports is 18.5 (Harvey, 2006), reports reduced to a reading level of grade 6 significantly improve parents' comprehension of information (Wedding, 1984). Supervisors can encourage trainees to meet this expectation by training them to reduce jargon, avoid colloquialisms, use a well-organized format, and effectively use tables to present results. The field of education is filled with an endless number of acronyms (e.g., IEP, RtI, BIP) and catch phrases. Even regular use of these terms between school professionals can cause miscommunication and leave parents and students who do not speak this "language" utterly confused. Trainees need to learn how to write their reports using clear behavioral terms (e.g., "child has difficulty maintaining attention" vs. "child has impaired executive functioning").

The report should also be organized so that there are clear links among referral, assessment, and intervention, ultimately serving as a reader-friendly document. We recommend that supervisors emphasize the use of well-developed referral questions that guide the evaluation, well-designed tables to present assessment results, and meaningful recommendations. Organizing the report around specific referral questions will help introduce the reader to the purpose of the evaluation. We have reviewed far too many reports that offer vague reasons for referral, including statements such as "this evaluation was conducted as part of the student's triennial evaluation." Including tables that are well designed and appropriately referenced helps to summarize the information concisely for parents and teachers. Tabled scores should include a clear statement of the degree of measurement error associated with each score, classification level, and information on how to interpret scores (Standard 13.14, Standards for Educational & Psychological Testing). That is, scores reported should be accompanied by confidence intervals, percentile ranks, and a descriptive category for each score. Age and grade equivalents may also help parents and teachers understand how the student performs when compared to peers. Recommendations are the "so what?" of the report and offer the reader guidance about the practical implications of the evaluation. Hass and Carriere (2014) advocate for writing recommendations that link specifically to student need with the following framework in mind: (a) additional evaluation, (b) accommodations, (c) instructional or curriculum modifications, (d) specialized supports or services, and (e) referrals to community agency or other resources.

Supervision activities to support summarizing written results

Learning how to write a concise and consumer friendly report is time consuming. Experienced practitioners are much more fluent in the report writing process than novice school psychologists who take about 6 to 8 hours to write a comprehensive psychological report (Whitaker, 1994). Practicum supervisors can support trainees with report writing by helping them first learn to budget their time. Supervisors should develop a plan for the writing and review process that considers time for an initial draft, supervisor review, trainee revision, and final submission of the report well in advance of the trainee's first assigned report. Supervisors and trainees should also discuss the processes for sharing drafts (e.g., use of track changes, use of written feedback) and reviewing feedback (e.g., verbal, written, or both) so that all expectations are clear. In the early stages of report writing, supervisors should also expect that some trainees may need to go through the review and revision process multiple times before the final product meets supervisor expectations. The length and nature of this process will change as the trainee gains competence and experience with report writing through the year. Most National Association of School Psychologists (NASP)-approved programs require students to complete at least one comprehensive psycho-educational report as part of their curriculum for reporting purposes (NASP, 2000). However, most districts only require a multidisciplinary report generated by the information management system be provided to parents and the team.

Once a basic process for report writing is established, the supervisor and supervisee should review expectations for the overall structure of the report. This is likely best achieved by sharing a number of sample reports with the trainee. It may also be quite useful to provide the trainee with a rubric or checklist of items that should be included in the report. An example checklist is provided in Handout 3.1 developed as part of a workshop on report writing for practitioners in the field (Kelly & Losoff, 2013). An excellent supervision activity is to ask supervisees to use this checklist to evaluate both the sample reports provided to gain familiarity with the tool and later for self-assessment when they write their first draft. For example, a supervisor may request that the trainee submit a self-assessment using the checklist along with the first draft so that the supervisor knows the trainee has completed close editing of his or her work before submission.

It is important that supervisees be provided opportunities to compile multiple sources of data in written format that would be understandable and useful for parents, teachers, administrators, and other relevant staff. One of the primary challenges for the novice supervisee is learning to use data to inform parents and teachers about what results mean and how they are reflected in a resulting IEP. At this stage, students are often more comfortable using scores and test manual language or templates to describe performance. Supervisors can assist supervisees by helping them determine whether an individual student is discrepant from his or her peers, therefore documenting "the need" for specialized services. Resources such as common core standards, state standards, and local norms may be useful tools for identifying the "norm."

We think that most supervisors would agree that report writing during practicum is time consuming for the trainee and equally so for the supervisor. Supervisors are ultimately responsible for the final evaluation report and written product. In many cases, it will become part of a student file. Many supervisors have shared that they spend hours editing, reviewing, and sometimes even writing portions of the report during the process. We feel that supervisors can lighten this burden and promote trainee growth by using a more active approach to the revision process. First, supervisors can ask that trainees check the readability index of their reports using Microsoft Word and try to improve the comprehension of their reports before submitting the

HANDOUT 3.1   General Report Checklist

Check if Criteria Is Met	Criteria
	General Content
	Included a reason for referral that is descriptive enough that someone unfamiliar with the case would understand why the student is referred
	Included referral questions
	Included a rationale for why some domains were not addressed (e.g., student scores in the average range for math)
	Explained each person's role (e.g., Mrs. Brown, Johnny's math teacher)
	Included mention of collaborators (e.g., other people gathering information)
	Acknowledged outside evaluation, if appropriate
	Described every assessment tool (e.g., what it measures, timed/untimed, computerized/paper and pencil, number of items, scoring, norms) so that someone who is unfamiliar with the tool would know what it is
	Linked each assessment with the referral question
	Used two to three sources of data to support each interpretation
	Described every intervention
	Included information that indicates that interventions are research based
	Explained the meaning of standardized scores (included classification descriptors)
	Included confidence intervals
	Organization
	Grouped assessments of similar content together
	Made sure that report is reader-centered
	Used clear, descriptive headings to guide the reader
	Included summaries for each section and/or an overall summary of all results

(continued)

HANDOUT 3.1 General Report Checklist (*continued*)

Check if Criteria Is Met	Criteria
	Grammar/APA Style
	Checked for spelling errors
	Checked for grammatical errors
	Wrote out all acronyms the first time they appear (e.g., CBM, ISAT, RtI, MAP, AE, PST, GET)
	Made sure active voice is used (e.g., teachers collected data vs. data were collected; the school psychologist administered the test vs. the test was administered)
	Checked to make sure there are no other student's names in the report
	Used correct pronouns throughout report (he/she, him/her)
	Made sure to use jargon-free descriptions
	Tables and Charts (APA Manual, 6th Ed.)
	Made sure that charts and tables are simple, clear, and free of extraneous detail
	Made sure that all tables and charts could stand alone (e.g., contained enough information that someone could interpret them without reading the rest of the report)
	Made sure that charts and tables had titles that were descriptive of the content
	Made sure that all tables had headings on every column and row
	Made sure that all charts and tables were referenced in the text
	Made sure that all elements in the chart were labeled clearly
	Made sure that the magnitude and scale in the chart made sense
	Made sure to include error of measurement (CIs), percentile ranks, and descriptive categories with all scores

Source: Kelly and Losoff (2013).

first draft. Box 3.1 provides instruction for using this function in Microsoft Word. We also recommend that supervisors do not use their red pen to line edit each draft of a supervisee's report. This is incredibly time-consuming and also limits the supervisee's ability to learn how to write independently. Supervisors should consider using a process such as the "minimal marking" method (Haswell, 1983). In this method, the reviewer places an "x" next to any line where they find "lower order" concerns (e.g., grammatical errors, misspellings, punctuation mistakes, poor sentence structure) and asks the writer to go back and find and fix each mistake. A similar approach would be to finely edit and revise one or two paragraphs of the report and ask the trainee to use this feedback to make similar changes throughout the document before further review. Another helpful activity is editing draft reports using different colored highlighters to highlight the information written about the student being evaluated in one color and the information written about the tests in a different color. This can help the supervisee identify how much of the report is about test scores or other data collection and how much is about the interpretation of individual student performance. This can result in a helpful talking tool about developing reports to better emphasize and describe individual student performance. A helpful supervisor reported that he has done this activity both as a side-by-side activity, as well as at different times and then making time to compare drafts. The end result is more efficiency in the process and more meaningful training for the supervisee.

Note on information management systems

Our experience working across many different districts and in several different states has informed us that much of the "paperwork" related to special education is now being stored using information management systems and/or databases (e.g., easyIEP, eIEP-pro, iep online). From a training perspective, the widespread use of information management systems to support compliance can make the process of report writing and IEP development look like the same activity when they are, in fact, distinct activities meant to complement, and inform, each other. Supervisors working in districts that

---

BOX 3.1   Instructions for Checking Readability Index of Reports

In Microsoft Word
Click the **File** tab, and then click **Options**.
Click **Proofing**.
Under **When correcting spelling and grammar in Word**, make sure the **Check grammar with spelling** check box is selected.
Select **Show readability statistics**.

utilize information management system should therefore take time to help supervisees understand how the written report relates to the information stored in online student records and how recommendations are reflected into meaningful IEP goals.

Presenting evaluation results

School-based evaluations require a multidisciplinary approach, whereby all relevant student domains (e.g., cognitive/intellectual, social/emotional, communication) that are potentially impacting student performance are assessed. These results are shared after evaluation via the IEP meeting and integrated into a working plan for the student (i.e., IEP). Parents, teachers, related service personnel, and others invited share important information and data during the meeting, often within a rather limited time period (e.g., 1 hour). Teams are often challenged to use time efficiently during the meetings, as time needs to be allocated for the presentation of results; the determination of eligibility, when relevant; the development of the IEP; and identification of placement and related services. At times, this may leave an estimated 5 to 10 minutes for one professional to present his or her evaluation results. Practicum supervisees have likely had very limited experience in paring down a presentation to a few key details and will require much practice with making their oral reports concise and user friendly.

Activities to support presenting evaluation results

A novice supervisee may be tempted to read every area of their written report and comment on every single test score without regard for understanding by parents or other staff. Supervisees need to learn to identify key results and then deliver them to others in a way that is easy to understand. This is perhaps best accomplished by providing several opportunities to practice. Supervisors can first have trainees practice by summarizing the most important data in a short handout or written outline. Next, supervisors should prompt trainees to practice presenting these "talking points" orally in advance of the first few meetings. A structured framework for reporting in meetings is included in Handout 3.2. Supervisors and trainees may find this resource helpful in preparing for the oral presentation in meetings during the early stages of training.

During meetings, supervisors should also provide additional support for trainees. This may start by first introducing the trainee to the team and explaining the supervisee's role in the meeting. For example, a supervisor may note that the practicum trainee conducted several portions of the evaluation of a student and is prepared to share those results with the team.

HANDOUT 3.2   Guidelines for Oral Reporting in Team or IEP Meetings

Directions: The purpose of these guidelines is to offer a framework for orally presenting results in team and IEP meetings in a concise and meaningful format. Users are encouraged to follow each step to create a one to two page summary form that will be used for reference during the oral report in the meeting. The summary form may be shared with team members or used only by the individual evaluator as an aid for reporting the information.

Step 1: Review Referral Concern/Questions
List and state referral concerns/questions: "I conducted this evaluation to address three specific referral questions. The first question is what is Sam's current level of achievement in reading ..."

Step 2: Review Assessment Tools Used in Evaluation
List and state specific assessment instruments used in evaluation: "To address these questions, I interviewed Mrs. Green, Sam's parents, assessed his reading skills with curriculum-based measurement and the WIAT-III, conducted two classroom observations, and ...."

Step 3: Highlight Assessment Results From Each Tool Used in Evaluation
List key assessment results from each assessment with bullet points and be sure to orient team members to important tables and graphs during the oral presentation. Also help the team members understand the results by placing them in the context of the classroom. "If you look at the Table on page 2 of the report, you can see that Sam performed in the average range in all areas on the WIAT-III except in the area of the Oral Reading Fluency .... Sam's difficulties

(continued)

in oral reading fluency impact his ability to read text accurately and quickly. For example, during assessment, Sam would often pause and get stuck on the initial sound of certain words." (*Note:* It is not useful to report all scores and data. You should summarize the assessment results and highlight information that is relevant to the student's current functioning.)

[Pause here and ask if anyone has questions about the results that were presented.]

Step 4: Provide Brief Interpretation of Evaluation Results
Provide a concise interpretation of evaluation results that highlights the original referral concern/questions, key assessment findings, and how this is translated into classroom performance. "I conducted this evaluation to address questions about Sam's reading abilities and results from teacher and parent interviews, classroom observations, and some additional testing revealed that Sam ...."

Step 5: Review Recommendations
Offer meaningful educational recommendations that are linked directly to assessment results. "To address Sam's decoding difficulties, I recommend that classroom staff provide ..."

Step 6: Open for Questions
Indicate the end of your presentation and ask team members if anyone has questions about the information or recommendations presented. You may also offer to make yourself available after the meeting if anyone would like to ask questions at a later time or in an individual meeting. "This is all I prepared to share in our meeting today, but I want to make sure to answer any questions you may have at this time about the information or recommendations I reviewed."

The supervisor will also want to keep close attention on the trainee's ability to convey this information effectively and monitor any anxiety that may limit the trainee. Supervisors may provide additional prompts, take time to clarify information for the team, and assist the trainee when there is any breakdown in communication.

After the meeting, supervisors should take time to debrief with the supervisee. The supervisor may consider beginning this conversation by asking the trainee to share his or her impressions of the meeting and performance. Supervisors should also be sure to offer positive comments on trainee strengths and identify any areas for improvement in subsequent meetings. Feedback provided about meetings can also be recorded and monitored for growth.

Fulfilling Other Team Roles

School psychologists can fulfill other roles defined by IDEIA. In many districts or LEAs, the school psychologist often functions as the district representative, charging them with the person knowledgeable about the district's resources and services. The skills required for this role come from the specific training that school psychologists receive in consultation and collaboration, as well as data-based decision making. While it would not be appropriate for a practicum trainee to engage in this activity, a supervisor can help facilitate the development of these skills by giving the supervisee practice at defining a student's needs and providing information about all of the district services that can be used to meet a specific need.

Another position in the special education process that school psychologists often fill is the role of case manager. No specific language in IDEIA identifies who can or cannot fulfill this responsibility. While typically a special education teacher or someone who engages in direct service delivery (e.g., speech-language teacher [SLP]) serves as the case manager, some districts assign this role to a school psychologist, especially if there are identified behavioral or mental health needs. The purpose of the case manager is usually to coordinate services and communication, serve as the point of contact with families and providers, manage IEP processes, schedule regular meetings, and report on progress. Again, this is a prime opportunity for a supervisor to help a trainee connect assessment with IEP services by coordinating progress reports or other documents. This also gives a trainee exposure to issues related to compliance with special education laws and regulations. An effective supervisor allows the supervisee to play a meaningful role from start to finish of the identification process, even if this may not be a day-to-day function of the school psychologist.

ROLE IN DEVELOPMENT OF THE INDIVIDUAL EDUCATION PLAN

Two NASP standards explicitly state that school psychologists enhance "the cognitive and academic skills" and "the development of wellness, social skills, mental health, and life competencies" of students (Ysseldyke et al., 2006). School psychologists are thus integral in developing meaningful interventions that improve student academic, social/emotional, and behavioral skills in school settings. Once a student has been identified as eligible for special education services, the district or LEA personnel use evaluation results to identify both the services and placement that will provide the student an LRE (Bateman & Linden, 2012). Supervisors should provide an understanding of how services are identified (IEP development) and how these services are delivered (placement) in their particular district, with an explicit understanding that "what" a student needs is identified before "where" the services will be delivered. Many, many misconceptions exist about special education and supervisors should take care in helping trainees understand that special education is about services and not "a place" where students spend all, or part, of their day. Supervisors should consider reviewing the following with supervisees to assist with understanding individualization: (a) how each disability category is defined by the particular state, (b) eligibility criteria, (c) the types of special services and instruction available, (d) which service personnel deliver services and instruction, (e) how length and intensity of time is determined, (f) how progress is documented, and (g) how services are decreased and increased over time. An emphasis on a continuum of services rather than a specific type based on a "label" will be helpful for a beginning practitioner. Special topics in special education, such as early childhood education, alternative and residential placements, and adult transition planning, may also be applicable, depending on a supervisor's caseload and assignment.

Activities to Support IEP Goal Development

Comprehensive evaluation reports include meaningful recommendations based on the assessment data gathered via the case study. Not all recommendations are integrated into the student IEP, but several may align directly to annual goals for the student. Supervisors should thus take time to orient practicum trainees to the practice of developing measurable goals and objectives linked to the evaluation report.

One activity that can be helpful is to direct the supervisee to review current IEPs to understand the reporting requirements and style of a particular state or district. Supervisors will want to orient trainees to particular portions of each IEP, including, but not limited to, where the following are documented: (a) current assessment results, (b) present levels of performance (PLOP), (c) annual goals, (d) related services, (e) placement, and (f) test accommodations. To provide practice, supervisors should prompt trainees to develop data-based goals and objectives after each evaluation. These goals can be documented as an exercise or in a separate report, if this is not a typical responsibility of the school psychologist (e.g., the case manager is responsible for goal development). A format and checklist for this activity is provided in Handout 3.3.

Supervision Activities to Understand School District Services

All students with special education needs are entitled to individualized services, which include "related services, supplementary aids and services, modifications, personnel support, and accommodations" (Bateman & Linden, 2012) delivered in the LRE. Supervisors can promote trainee understanding of individualized services by prompting the supervisee to cross reference the 13 federal disability categories with the state regulations and the district eligibility and placement procedures. In addition to understanding the "pathway" to specialized services, supervisees may benefit from observing a variety of special education settings and services in the district. For example, a supervisee may more readily translate "minutes of service" by shadowing a service provider and observing how services are delivered and documented. Supervisors may provide supervisees with access to other schools that house different types of special programming, especially for students with more intensive or low-incidence disabilities. This may include having supervisees shadow other supervisors or teachers in special population programming. A continuum of special education supports is described in Handout 3.4. This tool can be used in supervision to review the range of services provided in the district, discuss where and how they are delivered, and arrange for visits or observations.

HANDOUT 3.3   Writing Meaningful Instructional Recommendations and Annual Goals

_____ Recommendations reflect assessment results

_____ Recommendations are specific and could be implemented

_____ Recommendations are measurable

_____ Recommendations reflect a direction

_____ Recommendations are understandable and include environmental and instructional information

GOAL PLANNING FORM

Present Levels of Performance	Special Education, Related Services, and Supplemental Aids and Services	Measurable Annual Goals With Benchmark

HANDOUT 3.4 Continuum of Special Education Support and Services

General Education With Support
- Supplementary Services
  - Assistive technology devices
  - Instructional practices
  - Behavior intervention/support
  - Instructional adaptations
  - Curriculum accommodations
  - Curriculum modifications
  - Individualized supports
- Related Services
  - Speech or hearing
  - Occupational therapy
  - Physical therapy
  - Nursing or health
  - Mobility
  - Counseling
- Special Education Instruction
  - Specially designed and/or supplemental instruction to support the participation of the student with a disability in the general education classroom
  - Consultation with the student's general education teacher
  - Collaborative team teaching

Special Class Services
- School district schools/high schools, district supported specialized schools, state-operated/supported and approved nonpublic schools
- Provide intensive and specialized instruction and/or behavioral support
- May be provided on a part-time or full-time basis
- Characterized by smaller staff/student ratios, intensity of needs, specialization of curriculum and instruction, homogeneity of disabilities

Nonpublic Placement
- Meets the intensive educational or clinical needs of students who cannot be accommodated in a public school setting
- Highly restrictive
- Includes day schools and residential schools

Home or Hospital Placement
- Provides instruction for students who are unable to attend public or private school due to ongoing health or psychological needs that cannot be met in a school setting

EVALUATION OF THE SUPERVISEE

As noted in Chapter 2, supervisors should regularly review the supervisee's training plan and ensure that activities and goals are being addressed in the early stages of the practicum. Regular monitoring of the plan may include monthly or even more frequent reviews. Frequent review serves as an excellent way to formatively assess the supervisee in training. After the first few months in training, supervisors may also be required to conduct a more summative evaluation as part of the trainee's university requirements. Supervisors should pay particular attention to the trainee's readiness for advancement in training and to learning more advanced skills.

If the supervisee conducted a self-evaluation of his or her skills earlier in the year, it may be an excellent time to prompt the trainee to revisit this assessment and note where he or she has made progress and areas of continued need. Allowing the supervisee to complete the self-assessment first may encourage a more open and honest discussion regarding strengths and weaknesses during supervision. Supervisors may also find it easier to deliver difficult feedback or provide more targeted direction, particularly if the trainee's impressions are consistent with the supervisor's evaluation. Supervisees may also be more receptive to feedback from supervisors once they have had time to consider their own strengths and weaknesses. Particular attention should also be given to the types of activities and experiences the supervisee has gained during the training thus far.

SUPERVISOR TO-DO LIST

☐ Provide access to district special education compliance resources
☐ Plan for writing and editing multiple drafts of reports
☐ Allow practice for any team meeting or data presentations
☐ Plan for developing and/or writing IEP goals linked to evaluation data
☐ Arrange access to different types of programming
☐ Summative (if required) and/or formative assessment of supervisee's skill level and progress toward practicum plan goals

REFERENCES

Bateman, B., & Linden, M. (2012). *Better IEPs: How to develop legally correct and educationally useful programs* (5th ed.). Verona, WI: Attainment Company.

Brown-Chidsey, R., & Andren, K. J. (2013). *Assessment for intervention: A problem-solving approach.* New York, NY: The Guilford Press. Retrieved from /z-wcorg/

Castillo, J. M., Curtis, M. J., & Gelley, C. (2012). School psychology 2010: School psychologists' professional practices and implications for the field—Part 2. *NASP Communiqué*, *40*(7), 28–30.

Harvey, V. S. (2006). Variables affecting the clarity of psychological reports. *Journal of Clinical Psychology*, *62*(1), 5–18. doi:10.1002/jclp.20196

Hass, M. R., & Carriere, J. A. (2014). *Writing useful, accessible, and legally defensible psychoeducational reports.* Hoboken, NJ: Wiley.

Haswell, R. H. (1983). Minimal marking. *College English*, *45*(6), 600–604. Retrieved from http://www.jstor.org/stable/377147

Individuals with Disabilities Education Improvement Act, 20 U.S.C. § 1400 (2004).

Kelly, K. K., & Losoff, R. C. (2013, December). *Legally defensible psycho-educational reports.* Professional development workshop for school psychologists in the North Shore School District 112.

National Association of School Psychologists. (2000). *Standards for training and field placement programs in school psychology.* Bethesda, MD: Author.

Pelco, L. E., Ward, S. B., Coleman, L., & Young, J. (2009). Teacher ratings of three psychological report styles. *Training and Education in Professional Psychology*, *3*(1), 19–27. doi:10.1037/1931-3918.3.1.19

Sattler, J. M. (2001). *Assessment of children: Cognitive applications.* San Diego, CA: Jerome M. Sattler, Publisher.

Wedding, R. R. (1984). Parental interpretation of psychoeducational reports. *Psychology in the Schools*, *21*, 477–481.

Whitaker, D. (1994). *How school psychology trainees learn to communicate through the school psychological report.* Unpublished doctoral dissertation, University of Washington, Seattle, WA.

Ysseldyke, J. E., Burns, M., Dawson, P., Kelley, B., Morrison, D., Ortiz, S., … Telzrow, C. (2006). *School psychology: A blueprint for training and practice III.* Bethesda, MD: National Association of School Psychologists.

FOUR

WORKING IN A SCHOOL SYSTEM

While the focus of previous chapters has been on developing the skills necessary to work with individual students, mostly within the special education context, school psychologists also take on roles to develop systems of support, both preventive and responsive. The focus of this chapter is to help identify ways to help trainees develop a broader understanding of the different types of systems school psychologists interact with and how to develop meaningful trainee experiences.

MULTITIERED SYSTEMS OF SUPPORT

The 2001 reauthorization of the Education and Secondary Education Act (ESEA), also known as "No Child Left Behind," emphasized school accountability for student achievement, with the expectation that all students in grades 3 to 8 would be reading and math proficient within 12 years. This intensive focus on accountability, high-stakes testing, evidence-based practice, and the need for schools to demonstrate adequate achievement for all students provides an opportunity for school psychologists to broaden their service delivery role in the form of prevention (Ysseldyke et al., 2006).

To address this new approach to increasing student achievement, the 2006 National Association of School Psychologists (NASP) Blueprint and resulting 2010 practice model described competence in two areas as the standard for all practice (Armistead & Smallwood, 2014). The first outcome is to improve competence for all students including academic competencies (e.g., reading, math, science) and social-emotional competencies (e.g., social competence, problem solving). The second outcome is building systems capacity to sustain effective instruction and services for all students.

To support this shift from a focus on individuals, often utilizing a special education approach, schools and school psychologists apply a prevention model similar to a public health model of prevention and intervention. In this system, solutions are generated based on the "health" of the whole group or population and risk factors, such as underachievement, are identified early while the intensity of the solution or "treatment" is defined by the severity of the problem or known risk factor (Gresham, 2007). This approach in education is known as multitiered systems of support (MTSS) where the "tiers" represent interventions that serve smaller numbers of students as the intensity increases.

According to Stoiber (2014), MTSS refers to a "multicomponent, comprehensive, and cohesive school-wide and classroom-based positive support system through which students at risk for academic and behavioral difficulties are identified and provided with evidence-based and data-informed instruction, support, and intervention" (p. 45). The common features of all MTSS include using data to make decisions, using known effective practices or interventions, and evaluating progress. Moreover, a true systems approach utilizes an ecological perspective where student development is viewed as occurring within different environments including community systems, family systems, and social and political systems (Bronfenbrenner, 1986). How school professionals create and organize system-based solutions varies greatly and it would be impossible to describe a "right way." A common approach is to identify teams (e.g., problem-solving team [PST], behavior support team) to solve problems (e.g., low achievement, behavior problems) specific to the setting. These teams are created to both prevent and reduce the ultimate impact of individual student difficulties. Within MTSS, primary prevention services are implemented at the general education level to support all students. Simultaneously, targeted and intensive supports (secondary and tertiary level) are provided to at-risk and high-risk students. School psychologists engage in specific activities at each level of an MTSS.

School-Based Prevention and Intervention Supervision Activities

Practicum candidates will benefit from a basic introduction to site-specific prevention and intervention activities early in the training. This may include a review of the basic processes and structures the site has in place to support student academic and behavioral achievement, as well as the school psychologist's role in these processes. In particular, supervisors should orient trainees to specific school-wide practices (e.g., benchmark assessment procedures, tiered interventions, student identification practices) and structures (e.g., teams, manuals, data systems) used for

TABLE 4.1   Checklist for MTSS Activities
☐ Identify different prevention practices being used at the district and school level ☐ Identify team structure and roles at the district and school level ☐ Identify team activities at the district and school level ☐ Identify delivery of tiered services at the district and school level ☐ Identify data screening and monitoring practices at the district and school level ☐ Identify data decision-making process at the district and school level

prevention and intervention. Novice trainees may be easily confused by the various names and acronyms (e.g., RtI, PBIS) used for different MTSS practices. Supervisees should understand that because a school may not have an "RtI" or "PBIS" brand name team or initiative, there may very likely be systems or structures in place to prevent and intervene with student difficulties. For the purpose of this section, we have chosen to focus on preventing reading failure and challenging behaviors, two common initiatives in schools. It is important to emphasize that schools may also use a systems approach to focus on other academic areas such as math, writing, and English/Language Arts and other school-based initiatives (e.g., social-emotional, family engagement). We have also included a list of suggested supervision activities related to MTSS in Table 4.1.

MTSS Practices That Prevent Academic Failure

The focus on accountability has challenged school professionals to rethink, and redesign, academic instruction. Most school professionals recognize that students respond uniquely to instruction and have accepted that academic instruction must be differentiated for each learner. To accomplish this, school professionals often design a system of instruction following the MTSS framework for academic achievement. Within most systems, there are three tiers of instructional support. Tier 1 is the core curriculum provided to all students at the building level. Students who do not respond or make the expected rate of progress via academic measures receive additional Tier 2 group interventions, where they receive evidence-based instruction to address specific skill deficits in a given academic domain. A much smaller number of students who continue to demonstrate limited growth on academic measures, despite support through Tiers 1 and 2, receive intensive and targeted instruction to resolve significant skill deficits. School psychologists are very experienced with Tier 3 intervention support with its similarity to special education services, but are well equipped to assist with Tiers 1 and 2 practices as well.

Screening and monitoring practices

Universal screening is at the heart of identifying "responders" and "nonresponders" using data to make instructional decisions. School psychologists, with their foundational skills in assessment, play an important role in helping to support universal screening efforts. In addition to being reliable and valid (Salvia, Ysseldyke, & Bolt, 2010), effective screening measures incorporate the features of general outcome measures (GOMs) as first defined by Deno and others (Deno, 1985; Fuchs & Deno, 1991; Marston, 1989; McConnell, Priest, Davis, & McEvoy, 2002; Shinn, 2002, 2010). The GOM framework uses frequent measurement of specific indicators (i.e., fluency, digits correct, office referrals) to assess a larger outcome (i.e., reading, math, social skills) similar to a thermometer measuring body temperature as an indicator of overall health (Shinn, 2002). GOMs may be used to identify appropriate referrals for special education, evaluate student response to a particular intervention or instructional strategy (including pre-referral interventions), and determine whether a student is developing particular skills as expected (Fuchs & Deno, 1991). A full list of GOM features is included in Table 4.2. The commonly used dynamic indicators of basic early literacy skills (DIBELS), curriculum-based measures (CBMs), and individual growth and development indicators (IGDIs) are examples of GOMs.

Supervision activities for screening and monitoring

As part of the multitiered process, decisions about how students are achieving are made using data. Screening data help identify student need for intervention while monitoring data inform the effectiveness of the intervention. For example, school personnel may use measures of reading fluency in September to identify students for small group reading instruction. Another benchmark assessment, using the same fluency measures, may be conducted in October to determine if the students receiving intervention are improving at a rate that is expected. Supervisors should orient trainees to screening and

---

Table 4.2 General Outcome Measures (GOMs) Features.

- Measure an important growth outcome for young children
- Rely on "authentic" or natural child behaviors
- Sensitive to growth over time
- Sensitive to effects of intervention
- Inexpensive and easy to administer
- Standardized and replicable
- Technically adequate

progress monitoring practices used in the school. In some schools, students may largely be referred for support via a teacher- or parent-initiated process that may quickly result in an evaluation for special education eligibility. Other schools may offer a full range of tiered supports that are aligned to the screening and monitoring data gathered via school or district-wide practices. As an initial activity, a supervisee can identify the following assessment procedures: (a) school-based teams used to support academic achievement, (b) decision-making processes and activities, and (c) student referral and problem-solving processes. For example, a supervisee may identify that the school-based PST meets monthly to review reading data across all grade levels. Benchmark (screening) data are reviewed three times each year and progress monitoring data are reviewed bimonthly for students receiving intervention. Students receiving intensive Tier 3 intervention may be considered for additional evaluation or highly individualized programming (i.e., suspicion of a disability and referral for special education evaluation) after a specified period of time in Tier 3 services.

Curriculum and instructional design and delivery

Screening practices support the appropriate delivery of different instruction and/or interventions. As outlined in the Individuals With Disabilities Education Improvement Act (IDEIA; 2004), schools should provide instruction "based on scientific research" and any nonresponse is considered as part of any specific learning disability. Schools typically select from a number of commercially available reading programs that address the five areas of reading outlined by the National Reading Panel (NRP; 2000). In the vast majority of states, the Common Core State Standards Initiative also guides school curriculum objectives in all key academic areas. School psychologists should have a strong knowledge of the reading curriculum and instructional practice utilized within their district.

Supervision activities for tier 1, 2, and 3

School psychologists need to be critical consumers of research and able to readily identify evidence-based interventions for use in schools. At Tier 1, this requires that the school psychologist be able to assist school teams in identifying core curriculum for adoption. Supervisors can help trainees develop these skills by prompting them to examine the core academic curriculum at each grade level. Supervisees should identify both the supporting evidence and the process used in selection (e.g., teacher preference, committee review of literature). Supervisees may find resources such as the Institute of Education Sciences' *What Works Clearinghouse* (WWC) and the Education Resources Information Center (ERIC) helpful for this activity. The former is a source that provides information about the evidence of thousands of educational interventions, while the latter is an online library of education research and information. Other resources include *Best Evidence Encyclopedia* (www.bestevidence.org) and the *National Center on RtI Instructional Intervention Tools Chart* (www.rti4success.org/instructionTools). Supervisees may consider creating a curriculum resource that documents the core academic curriculum in reading, math, and writing and the evidence of effectiveness for each. This resource may serve as a helpful tool during training and the early stages of their professional career. The resource may also be a helpful tool for the field supervisor to maintain and share with other school personnel at the site. Worksheets for evaluating both academic and behavioral programs are included in Handouts 4.1 and 4.2.

Effective Tier 2 reading instruction is designed to provide more intensive, systematic instruction focusing on the five foundational skills of comprehension, vocabulary, phonemic awareness, fluency with text, and alphabetic principle (NRP, 2000). Intervention groups should meet three to four times each week for a minimum of 30 minutes (Burns & Gibbons, 2008). Supervisors may consider facilitating a number of activities to orient trainees to these activities, including the following: (a) participating in identification practices (e.g., "data days"), (b) participating in the selection of evidence-based reading programs aligned to student skill deficits, (c) providing intervention to a small group of students, and (d) assisting with the progress monitoring of Tier 2 services.

At least 14 states now require by law that a response-to-intervention (RtI) process is used in the identification of specific learning disabilities (SLD) (Response to Intervention Network, n.d.). Contemporary school psychologists, as such, must be prepared to use this process as part of an academic case study for nonresponders to Tier 2 and 3 interventions. Several training programs now also require school psychology candidates to demonstrate competence through the submission of academic and behavioral case studies using RtI methods. During the practicum, supervisors may help to prepare candidates for this more advanced case study. As an introductory activity, supervisors may prompt supervisees to practice identifying appropriate reading interventions for a relevant student case (e.g., student exhibiting reading difficulties). Haring and Eaton's (1978) instructional learning hierarchy is a useful tool aligned to student learning and skill development and may be helpful with this activity. A useful adaptation of this resource can be found at *http://www.interventioncentral.org/sites/default/files/pdfs/pdfs_interventions/IH_matrix.pdf*.

In addition to understanding how schools support achievement, it would also be beneficial for a supervisee to understand how a school responds to significant underachievement or "failure." Although not an evidence-based or promoted practice, retention is often a response to serious failure, either

HANDOUT 4.1   Worksheet for Evaluating Academic Programs

	Reading	Math	English and Language Arts (ELA)/ Writing
Program or practice			
Year and process for selection			
Source of evidence			
Describe how it addresses key areas or components: Reading: ■ Comprehension ■ Vocabulary ■ Phonics ■ Phonemic awareness ■ Fluency Math: Counting and cardinality (K, 1) Operations and algebraic thinking Number and operations in base 10 Number and operations—fractions Measurement and data Geometry			
Effectiveness data (includes description of population)			

Based on IRIS Module, *Evidence-Based Practices (Part 1): Identifying and Selecting a Practice or Program*. Key Instruction Shifts of the Common Core State Standards for Mathematics (pdf). Based on http://www.achievethecore.org/downloads/Math%20Shifts%20and%20Major%20Work%20of%20 Grade.pdf

HANDOUT 4.2   Worksheet for Evaluating Behavioral Programs

	Supporting Positive Behaviors	Reduction Strategies
Program or practice		
Year and process for selection		
Source of evidence for effectiveness		
Describe how it addresses key outcomes:		
Interpersonal skills		
Social functioning		
Social skills		
Problem solving		
Violence/aggression		
Substance abuse		
Other		
Effectiveness data (includes description of population)		

Based on IRIS Module, *Evidence-Based Practices (Part 1): Identifying and Selecting a Practice or Program*. Key Instruction Shifts of the Common Core State Standards for Mathematics (pdf). http://www.achievethecore.org/downloads/Math%20Shifts%20and%20Major%20Work%20of%20 Grade.pdf persistent failure on academic tasks or failing scores on state tests or other high-stakes activities. Districts and/or schools often have individual policies for retention and many states now require by law that students who do not meet proficiency on annual state achievement tests in third grade be retained. Retention can have serious costs, both emotionally and academically, for students so it is important for supervisees to understand when these decisions are made and what systemic supports are in place once a student has been retained (Jimerson, Anderson, & Whipple, 2002; Silberglitt, Jimerson, Burns, & Appleton, 2006).

Professional support and development

Credentialed school psychologists and other professional school personnel are required to engage in continuous professional development throughout their career. The National Staff Development Council defines professional development as a shared process of raising student achievement (National Staff Development Council, n.d.). The delivery of professional development varies by type and content but is usually delivered as a short course, seminar, workshop, online module, or presentation. Each state and professional organization (e.g., NASP, American Psychological Association [APA]) defines professional standards individually and provides license and/or certificate holders the standards for continued development and education. As part of this process, license/certificate holders earn continuing education units similar to a college credit system. For example, school psychologists holding National Certification in School Psychology (NCSP) are required to complete a minimum of 75 continuing professional development (CPD) activities within 36 months of renewal of the certification.

School districts provide a range of professional development activities each year to address both the credentialing needs of the school professionals working in the district and ultimately promote student achievement via best practices in education. Districts may also support ongoing professional development for school personnel by allocating time for collaboration among staff. This may be accommodated with occasional or even regular student release days throughout the school year. For example, students may start school 2 hours late every Thursday to allow time for teacher collaboration on new common core English and language arts standards.

Supervision activities for professional development

Supervisors should aim to facilitate and encourage trainees to take advantage of important professional development activities provided in the district during the practicum. Supervision activities in this area accomplish two objectives: (a) orient trainees to professional expectations as a future license/certificate holder, and (b) provide additional training in specific content areas. As an initial activity, supervisors may review the district professional development calendar with the trainee. During this review, it is important to highlight how each professional development activity is aligned to school and district improvement goals. For example, a district that has identified low achievement as an issue may offer a series of professional development activities related to evidence-based reading practice. Supervisors can then assist supervisees in identifying a list of activities that are appropriate and feasible for their training plan during the practicum.

Some supervising school psychologists also regularly provide professional development for other school staff as part of consultation and systems level activities. Supervisors should consider inviting practicum candidates to assist them or other staff in preparing professional development opportunities for other school staff. For example, a trainee may assist his or her supervisor in developing a presentation on classroom management for a group of paraprofessionals working in an elementary school. Supervisors who do not engage in these activities may consider connecting the trainee to other school professionals who may offer this experience. For example, a trainee may work with the school social worker to provide a parent education unit on structuring homework activities. These activities are aimed at the supervisee gaining experience in planning, designing, and presenting content to an adult audience.

MTSS Practices That Promote Positive Behavior

School professionals have long recognized that academic success is intimately tied to behavioral competence and that challenging behaviors negatively impact student success. Prevention-oriented practices such as School-wide Positive Behavioral Interventions and Supports (SWPBIS) promote prosocial behaviors in the same way that academic prevention approaches target achievement. SWPBIS is a framework for providing a multitiered level of supports that promote prosocial behavior while preventing problem behaviors. At the heart of SWPBIS is a commitment to creating a positive school culture aimed at promoting social competence and academic achievement. The model includes four key elements: (a) the selection of relevant academic and behavior *outcomes*; (b) evidence-based *practices* to support those outcomes; (c) *data* to identify needs, make decisions, and monitor progress; and (d) *systems* to support sustainable implementation.

As a complement to prevention-focused disciplinary practices, some schools also implement social and emotional learning (SEL) programs aimed at increasing social competence. The Collaborative for Academic, Social, and Emotional Learning (CASEL) has identified five core affective, behavioral, and cognitive competencies: self-awareness, self-management, social awareness, relationship skills, and responsible decision making. These competencies are directly related to an individual's ability to feel and manage emotions, feel and show empathy, solve problems, develop and maintain relationships, make decisions, and set positive goals (CASEL, n.d.). Competence in these five areas results in use of positive social behavior, academic success, and fewer negative outcomes such as conduct problems and emotional distress (CASEL, n.d.). A few states (Illinois, Kansas, Pennsylvania, and West Virginia) have identified specific SEL standards and have incorporated them into required standards or benchmarks. Schools interested in implementing an SEL program may choose from a variety of commercially available and evidence-based programs. The *2013 CASEL Guide: Effective Social and Emotional Learning Programs—Preschool and Elementary School Edition* is an excellent source, as it provides a thorough review of well-designed, evidence-based SEL programs.

How schools support positive behavior varies slightly depending on the prevention framework (e.g., SWPBIS, SEL) or curriculum used (e.g., Second Step, Promoting Alternative Thinking Strategies [PATHS]). A number of approaches exist but all share several common features. Effective teaching of prosocial behavior includes (a) agreed upon expectations for positive behavior, (b) agreed upon definitions of expectations for positive behavior, (c) consistent teaching and support for the expectations of positive behavior, (d) multiple tiers of intervention, and (e) screening and monitoring systems in place to measure the behaviors and response to instruction.

Supervision activities for curriculum and school-wide practices

As an introduction to school-wide behavior supports, supervisors can first orient trainees to school-wide behavioral expectations. Supervisees should identify building and classroom rules and examine how they are taught and reinforced in various school settings. Trainees who are placed in a school using SWPBIS should find this information more readily available, as well as visible, in the school. For example, a supervisee may find the school rules of *Be Safe, Be Respectful*, and *Be Prepared* posted in the school halls and classrooms during a quick tour of the school. The trainee may also observe school staff teaching the expectations with demonstrations in relevant school settings (e.g., hallways, cafeteria, and playground) during the first few weeks of school and subsequently observe staff reinforce student prosocial behavior with a special token. Trainees that are placed in schools that do not implement SWPBIS may find that reading the student handbook or discipline code a good place to begin their review. Supervisors may consider creating a scavenger-type activity to help orient trainees to discipline and behavior support practices.

Supervisors can also orient trainees to any social emotional or behavioral curriculum available for use or implemented in classrooms or small groups. Some supervisors may find it helpful to connect the trainee to other support staff, such as the school social worker or counselor, if they do not have an active role with the implementation of SEL practices. Supervisees should be encouraged to evaluate the evidence supporting each program as well. The WWC, CASEL, and the National Registry for Evidence-Based Programs and Practices (NREPP) all provide information about the effectiveness of evidence-based practices and programs. A basic process for reviewing these practices is included in Handout 4.2. Supervisees should also be oriented to any reduction or punishment strategies used in the school to address serious problem behaviors. Although all prevention programs promote the use of effective and positive approaches to addressing problem behavior, many schools incorporate some level of punishment-oriented strategies (e.g., detention, verbal reprimand, time out) as part of the school-wide approach to discipline.

Supervision activities for screening and monitoring

Practicum trainees should be oriented to any behavioral data that are used within the school site for student identification, decision making, and progress monitoring. Supervisors should take time to orient trainees to the data collection systems in place within classrooms and at the building level. These may include a range of behavioral indicators, such as homework completion, attendance, and office referrals, to name a few. Office discipline referrals (ODRs) are a widely used measure in many schools to evaluate student behavior. Many schools will also purchase an account with the web-based School-Wide Information System (SWIS) to help collect, organize, and analyze student data. Other readily available tools include the Social Skills Improvement System (SSIS) and Behavioral and Emotional Screening System (BESS) as part of the AIMSweb Behavior tool. In the absence of commercially available resources, school professionals may also use other sources of data (e.g., detention records, suspension data) and data management tools (e.g., Microsoft Excel) to collect and analyze student behavior data. Supervisors may consider a number of activities to support trainee orientation to the behavior data in the school, including participation in benchmark assessment, data entry and analysis, and the preparation of data reports and graphs for team meetings. Many candidates are often proficient with computer programs such as Microsoft Excel and Word and may be quite helpful in organizing data, conducting basic analyses, and creating graphical representations of both individual student and school-wide data.

Tier 2 and 3 practices

Tier 2 interventions are typically delivered to groups of students exhibiting problem behaviors across multiple settings. Crone, Hawken, and Horner (2010) indicate the following critical features of Tier 2 interventions: (a) consistent, standardized implementation across students, (b) easily accessible, (c) continuous availability, (d) implemented by all school staff, and (e) provide extra doses of school-wide expectations and interventions. While a number of effective Tier 2 interventions exist, the check-in check-out (CICO) is a popular and well-research school-based intervention. Students participating in CICO set behavioral goals and work with a staff member or coach to monitor the goal, receive reinforcement when the goal is met, and communicate progress with the parent or caregiver (Cheney et al., 2010). Tier 3 interventions are highly individualized and matched to student needs based on data. Most often, this includes a functional behavior assessment (FBA) and resulting behavior intervention plan (BIP), but may also include resources such as individual counseling and consultation with multiple outside agencies in what is often referred to as "wrap-around" services.

Supervision activities for tiers 2 and 3

Supervisors should first orient practicum candidates to any Tier 2 practices implemented in the site. Supervisees may review district manuals and resources to help orient them to the practices. In addition, it may be quite helpful to facilitate activities that allow the trainee to observe interventions and eventually serve as an interventionist. For example, a trainee may observe the first four sessions of an 8-week small group intervention and colead the group with another school professional for the remaining meetings. Practicum candidates may also be in a unique position to contribute to intervention resources in the site via the training and support through their graduate program. Candidates may have access to packaged interventions through their university library or test kit center that they can share with the site for a specified period of time. School personnel may use these resources to pilot a particular program, while candidates gain valuable experience in intervention practice. Some candidates may also be required to design and/or implement behavioral interventions as part of a course. Supervisors should consider how to facilitate these activities for the candidate so that it enhances the candidate's training and benefits the school. For example, a supervisor may connect the trainee to the school behavior support team to design a new group-based intervention to address executive functioning deficits.

Supervisors should also help supervisees understand how FBAs are conducted and how BIPs are developed in their particular site. This includes an introduction to all required paperwork, district requirements for conducting the FBA and developing the BIP, and timelines for evaluation, intervention, and progress review. Some districts view the FBA strictly as a special education evaluation, while others broaden its use to any student who may benefit from highly individualized behavior support. Supervisors should also consider how to facilitate opportunities for the supervisees to be involved with the FBA and BIP process. Practicum candidates may be involved in a range of activities, including: (a) a review of current FBAs and BIPs in student files, (b) collecting relevant data for a supervisor FBA (e.g., student observations, teacher interview), (c) assisting with intervention development of a supervisor BIP, and (d) conducting a full FBA case study and designing a corresponding BIP. Some training institutions will require practicum candidates to conduct at least one FBA and design a corresponding BIP during the practicum. Field supervisors can assist by assigning the candidate to a relevant case, while university supervisors can assist by communicating clear expectations for the assignment.

Other Specific Prevention Practices

As a result of many significant and high-profile traumatic incidents in schools, there exists a body of knowledge that informs practitioners how to both prevent and respond to crisis situations. Crises may include natural disasters, such as a fire, flood, or tornado; a violent incident in the school (e.g., shooting); a pandemic of illness or infectious disease; or the death of a student or staff member. The NASP PREPaRE model is an excellent resource for schools and school psychologists in crisis prevention and intervention (Brock et al., 2009). Regardless of the particular approach, most school districts have an identified crisis plan, as required by state or local safety laws.

There are a number of additional school-based prevention programs that address specific issues, including those that target school failure, bullying, mental health, substance abuse, violence, and sex education, to name a few. Programs such as the *Olweus Bullying Prevention Program* (Olweus et al., 2007) and *Steps to Respect* (Committee for Children, 2001) specifically target bullying and violence prevention, respectively, and have been shown to reduce problematic behaviors (Felix, Sharkey, Green, Furlong, & Tanigawa, 2011).

Supervision activities to explore other prevention practices

A supervisee will hopefully never experience a crisis in his or her school setting and planning for a crisis would be beyond a practicum candidate's skill level. However, it would be beneficial for a supervisee to gain as much exposure to the school's plan and approach to responding to a crisis if an incident should occur. Most schools have a written, easily accessible crisis plan available for all school staff, which includes procedures for responding during a crisis and follow-up activities. A supervisee can review this plan in combination with literature on crisis prevention and intervention (e.g., NASP PREPaRE model) as an introductory activity. Supervisors may also try to coordinate opportunity for the supervisee to attend any crisis team meetings or staff training on crisis prevention during the practicum experience. If applicable, supervisees may also observe or participate in after-care counseling or debriefing following a critical incident. Mitchell and Everly (2001) provide critical incident debriefing techniques that may be used with students or staff who have been affected.

Family–School Collaboration

Collaboration with families is identified as an important feature of school-based prevention activities. The importance of involving parents in children's education is based on evidence that children perform most optimally in school when instructional, home, and school–family support for learning exists (Ysseldyke & Christenson, 2002). Domain 7 of the NASP practice model also explicitly recognizes the school psychologist's role in family–school collaboration services. While there are a number of effective practices for engaging families in education, a thorough discussion is beyond the scope of this book. It is important to highlight, however, that prevention is most effective when school personnel use a personal, high-touch approach that starts with creating a positive connection and communicating with family (Sheridan, Clarke, & Christenson, 2014). This is effective for two reasons: (a) it creates a common understanding of a student's skills and strengths, and (b) it allows for earlier and timely prevention or intervention. School psychologists should, therefore, find meaningful ways to engage families in all aspects of their work.

Supervision activities for family–school collaboration

Practicum candidates will benefit initially from a general introduction to school policies and practices targeted to involve parents. Supervisees may then identify specific activities that target parent involvement, such as parent–teacher conference, back to school activity, curriculum night, family fair, and community resource fair, a parent support group, and parent organizations (e.g., parent–teacher association [PTA]), to name a few. Supervisees can learn more about the home–school support strategies from many sources, not just their immediate supervisor. Supervisors may consider connecting the trainee to other school personnel who work closely with parents on a regular basis, such as the school social worker, classroom teachers, a parent liaison, school administrators, and administrative staff.

EVALUATION OF THE SUPERVISEE'S SKILL

Formal evaluation typically occurs at the end of the candidate's academic term with the university and most often using a university evaluation form. In a practicum that is designed for a full academic year, this first evaluation may be conducted at midyear (i.e., December) and designed as a formative assessment of a candidate's progress during the training. It is an ideal time for field supervisors to provide information about the trainee's strengths and limitations as a school psychologist-in-training. University supervisors should take time to clearly communicate with field supervisors about both how to use the evaluation tool and how information from the evaluation will be used in the candidate's training well in advance of the submission deadline. For example, low ratings on multiple areas on the evaluation may result in a remediation plan or a potential termination of the candidate's practicum training and require additional follow-up with the supervisor.

Results of the evaluation should be clearly shared with the supervisee and two supervising psychologists (i.e., field and university). This may be best achieved in a meeting, but may also be accomplished via communications between the pair (e.g., phone contacts, e-mail communications, and individual meetings). The two main goals for these communications are to (a) share the evaluation and clarify feedback, and (b) plan for the candidate's advancement in training. Planning for the trainee's advancement includes making a decision about continuation in the practicum (e.g., fit for site and readiness for field work), as well as identifying opportunities for growth in the training experience (e.g., new experiences and roles). We recommend that any new opportunities for growth discussed during the evaluation are further documented in an existing or new candidate training plan.

SUPERVISOR TO-DO LIST

☐ Provide access to district curriculum resources and processes
☐ Provide information and access to district or school screening assessment or decision-making processes
☐ Help facilitate access to develop or assist with individual interventions
☐ Provide district crisis response information or resources
☐ Provide resources or access to specific district prevention practices

REFERENCES

Armistead, R. B., & Smallwood, D. L. (2014). The national association of school psychologists' model of comprehensive and integrated school psychological services. In A. Thomas and P. Harrison (Eds.), *Best practices in school psychology: Data-based decision making* (pp. 9–24). Bethesda, MD: National Association of School Psychologists.

Brock, S. E., Nickerson, A. B., Reeves, M. A., Jimerson, S. R., Feinberg, T., & Lieberman, R. (2009). *School crisis prevention and intervention: The PREPaRE model*. Bethesda, MD: National Association of School Psychologists.

Bronfenbrenner, U. (1986). Ecology of the family as a context for human development: Research perspectives. *Developmental Psychology, 22*, 723–742.

Burns, M., & Gibbons, K. (2008). *Implementing RTI in elementary and secondary schools: Procedures to assure scientific-based practices*. New York, NY: Taylor & Francis.

Cheney, D., Lynass, L., Flower, A., Waugh, M., Iwaszuk, W., Mielenz, C., & Hawken, L. (2010). The check, connect and expect program: A targeted, tier 2 intervention in the schoolwide positive behavior support model. *Preventing School Failure, 54*(3), 152–158.

Collaborative for Academic and Social Emotional Learning. (n.d.). *CASEL—Success in schools, skills for life*. Retrieved from http://www.casel.org/

Committee for Children. (2001). *Steps to respect: A bullying prevention program*. Seattle, WA: Author.

Crone, D. A., Hawken, L. S., & Horner, R. H. (2010). *Responding to problem behavior in schools: The behavior education project* (2nd ed.). New York, NY: Guilford Press.

Deno, S. L. (1985). Curriculum-based measurement: The emerging alternative. *Exceptional Children, 52*(3), 219–232.

Felix, E., Sharkey, J., Green, J., Furlong, M., J. & Tanigawa, D. (2011). Getting precise and pragmatic about the assessment of bullying: The development of the California bullying victimization scale. *Aggressive Behavior, 37*, 234–247.

Fuchs, L. S., & Deno, S. L. (1991). Paradigmatic distinctions between instructionally relevant measurement models. *Exceptional Children, 57*, 488–500.

Gresham, F. (2007). Evolution of the response-to-intervention concept: Empirical foundations and recent developments. In S. R. Jimerson, M. K. Burns, & A. M. VanDerHeyden (Eds.), *Handbook of response to intervention: The science and practice of assessment and intervention* (pp. 10–24). New York, NY: Springer.

Haring, N. G., & Eaton, M. D. (1978). Systematic instructional procedures: An instructional hierarchy. In N. G. Haring, T. C. Lovitt, M. D. Eaton, & C. L. Hansen (Eds.), *The fourth R: Research in the classroom* (pp. 23–40). Columbus, OH: Merrill.

Individuals With Disabilities Education Improvement Act, 20 U.S.C. § 1400 (2004).

Jimerson, S. R., Anderson, G. E., & Whipple, A. D. (2002). Winning the battle and losing the war: Examining the relation between grade retention and dropping out of high school. *Psychology in the Schools, 39*(4), 441–457. doi:10.1002/pits.10046

Marston, D. B. (1989). A curriculum-based measurement approach to assessing academic performance: What it is and why do it. In M. R. Shinn (Ed.), *Curriculum-based measurement: Assessing special children* (pp. 18–78). New York, NY: Guilford Press.

McConnell, S. R., Priest, J. S., Davis, S. D., & McEvoy, M. A. (2002). Best practices in measuring growth and development in preschool children. In A. Thomas & J. Grimes (Eds.), *Best practices in school psychology IV* (Vol. 2, pp. 1231–1246). Bethesda, MD: National Association of School Psychologists.

Mitchell, J. T., & Everly, G. S., Jr. (2001). *Critical incident stress management: Basic group crisis interventions*. Ellicott City, MD: International Critical Incident Stress Foundation.

National Reading Panel. (2000). *Report of the national reading panel—teaching children to read: An evidence-based assessment of the scientific research literature on reading and its implications for reading instruction.* Washington, DC: National Institute of Child Health and Human Development.

National Staff Development Council. (n.d.). Retrieved from http://aypf.org/docu ents/62609NSDCDefinitionofProfessionalDevelopment908.pdf

Olweus, D., Limber, S. P., Flex, V., Mullin, N., Riese, J., & Snyder, M. (2007). *Olweus' bullying prevention program: Schoolwide guide.* Center City, MN: Hazelden.

Response to Intervention Network. (n.d.). The legal dimension of RTI: Part II. State laws and guidelines. Retrieved from http://www.rtinetwork.org/learn/ld/ the-legal-dimension-of-rti-part-ii-state-laws-and-guidelines

Salvia, J. S., Ysseldyke, J. E., & Bolt, S. (2010). *Assessment in special and inclusive education* (11th ed.). Boston, MA: Wadsworth/Cengage Publications.

Sheridan, S. M., Clarke, B. L., & Christenson, S. L. (2014). Best practices in promoting family engagement. In P. L. Harrison & A. Thomas (Eds.), *Best practices in school psychology: Systems level services* (pp. 439–454). Bethesda, MD; National Association of School Psychologists.

Shinn, M. R. (2002). Best practices in curriculum-based measurement and its use in a problem-solving model. In A. Thomas & J. Grimes (Eds.), *Best practices in school psychology IV* (pp. 671–698). Bethesda, MD: National Association of School Psychologists.

Shinn, M. R. (2010). Building a scientifically based data system for progress monitoring and universal screening across three tiers including RTI using curriculum-based measurement. In M. R. Shinn & H. M. Walker (Eds.), *Interventions for achievement and behavior problems in a three-tier model, including RTI* (pp. 259–293). Bethesda, MD: National Association of School Psychologists.

Silberglitt, B., Jimerson, S. R., Burns, M. K., & Appleton, J. J. (2006). Does the timing of grade retention make a difference? Examining the effects of early versus late retention. *School Psychology Review, 35,* 134–141.

Stoiber, K. C. (2014). A comprehensive framework for multi-tiered systems of support in school psychology. In P. L. Harrison & A. Thomas (Eds.), *Best practices in school psychology* (pp. 41–70). Bethesda, MD; National Association of School Psychologists.

Ysseldyke, J. E., & Christenson, S. L. (2002). *FAAB: Functional assessment of academic behavior: Creating successful learning environments.* Longmont, CO: Sopris West.

Ysseldyke, J. E., Burns, M., Dawson, P., Kelley, B., Morrison, D., Ortiz, S., … Telzrow, C. (2006). *School psychology: A blueprint for training and practice III.* Bethesda, MD: National Association of School Psychologists.

FIVE

MOVING TOWARD INDEPENDENCE

As discussed in Chapter 1, *novice trainees* are characterized as being highly motivated, having limited self-awareness, and focused on skill acquisition. Supervision activities in the early stages are likely to be highly structured and prescriptive and require close monitoring of skill development, as supervisees are more likely to be anxious and more dependent on their supervisors. As trainees demonstrate a basic level of proficiency in practice domains and any early anxiety decreases, it is an ideal time to consider more independence in the practicum setting. Doing so requires supervision around role expansion and important professional dispositions. Supervisors can help trainees to explore new school psychological roles, focus on professional behaviors that will help them gain independence, and develop a repertoire of self-care strategies. Each of these supervision issues is explored in this chapter.

EXPLORING NEW ROLES

The *National Association of School Psychologists (NASP) Model for Comprehensive and Integrated School Psychological Services* (NASP, 2010) outlines 10 practice domains for school psychologists. As the model suggests, the role of the contemporary school psychologist is broad, making the demands for preparing and training school psychology candidates complex. Practicum supervisors and supervisees can easily become overwhelmed by the breadth and depth of school psychology training expectations, particularly given the limited amount of time that candidates spend in practicum training (e.g., 2 days/week). In fact, some common questions field supervisors ask include "What should the supervisee do during the practicum?" "Is he or she doing enough?" and "What else should I have the supervisee do?" Supervisors are acutely aware of the training demands for school psychologists and some may even be a bit concerned about their ability to meet these demands in their field sites. Identifying both the opportunities and challenges that are unique to each site can help supervisors plan for the types of experiences they may facilitate during the practicum.

Understanding how the NASP practice domains relate to current practice is helpful in advancing this discussion. By and large, practicum candidates often do what their supervisors do! In a recent national survey of the field (Castillo et al., 2012), school psychologists reported engaging in the following activities most often: conducting psychoeducational evaluations (47%), providing student-focused consultation (10.4%), providing school-wide social emotional supports (10.8%), providing early intervention services (13.2%), and delivering interventions (23.2%). The reality is that most candidates will spend most of their time in the field engaging in similar activities. Supervisors may find it challenging to facilitate activities related to other practice domains because of the limitation of their own role in a particular district. We have oriented the supervision activities in the following section with this particular challenge in mind.

Supervision Activities to Support Role Expansion

Supervisors can support initial role expansion by merely allowing supervisees to conduct activities where they have already demonstrated proficiency with more independence. This may include having a trainee complete certain activities with less direct supervision or assigning the trainee slightly more advanced casework. For example, after directly observing a supervisee successfully complete consultation interviews with several teachers, a supervisor may direct the trainee to facilitate a new teacher consultation independently and reserve time during individual supervision sessions to provide support for the case. More advanced casework may mean that a supervisor assigns a more complex version of familiar casework (e.g., functional behavior assessment [FBA] for a child with multiple or more severe problem behaviors) to the supervisee.

Supervisors may also support trainee role expansion by assigning new activities and responsibilities, particularly in NASP domain areas that are underrepresented in current practice (e.g., counseling, systems-level consultation, family–school collaboration). We have developed a list of suggested activities that align with the 10 NASP domains and are relevant to the practicum experience. While this is not an exhaustive list of school psychological activities, supervisors may find that it serves as a helpful guide for ensuring that supervisees obtain a broad range of experiences during the practicum training. This resource is found in Table 5.1.

TABLE 5.1 Suggested Practicum Activities

NASP Practice Domain	Suggested Practicum Activities
Practices That Permeate All Aspects of Service Delivery	
Domain 1: Data-based decision making and accountability	1. Conduct case study evaluations 2. Develop data-driven interventions 3. Administer, score, interpret a variety of assessment measures: Curriculum-Based Measurement (CBM), authentic and portfolio assessment, traditional standardized assessment, observation codes and coding systems/techniques, play-based assessment, family assessment techniques, interview techniques, rating scales, informal assessment techniques, learning/instructional environment 4. Conduct record reviews 5. Propose individualized education program (IEP) goals, modifications, and academic strategies for teachers 6. Progress monitor interventions and treatment plans 7. Interview students, parents, and staff 8. Observe district curriculum meetings 9. Analyze classroom or grade level data 10. Conduct functional behavioral assessment (FBA) 11. Develop behavior intervention plan (BIP)
Domain 2: Consultation and collaboration	1. Consult with teachers using formal process/model 2. Participate in school improvement activities 3. Provide in-service training 4. Provide parent education 5. Collaborate about academic or behavioral interventions in class and educational placements with staff and parents 6. Collaborate with school staff and parents regarding IEP goals 7. Participate in IEP meetings 8. Participate in team meetings using the problem-solving model to screen at-risk students. 9. Provide academic or behavioral consultation with teachers and/or parents
Direct and Indirect Services for Children, Families	
Student-Level Services	
Domain 3: Interventions and instructional support to develop academic skills	1. Participate in problem-solving cases or on team 2. Develop instructional plans and IEP goals 3. Review evaluation techniques used in district 4. Develop appropriate recommendations based on assessment results 5. Develop transition plans 6. Interview student during problem-solving process

(continued)

TABLE 5.1 Suggested Practicum Activities (*continued*)	
NASP Practice Domain	**Suggested Practicum Activities**
	7. Practice keeping behavior logs
	8. Identify program modifications
	9. Develop effective academic interventions
	10. Review school/district curriculum
	11. Use CBM results to make suggestions for academic purposes
Domain 4: Interventions and mental health services to develop social and life skills	1. Develop effective behavior intervention techniques
	2. Consult with teachers and parents
	3. Implement interventions to achieve student behavioral or emotional goals
	4. Collaborate with colleagues regarding IEP goals
	5. Use research-based interventions
	6. Conduct FBA and collaborate with teachers, parents, and students
	7. Develop BIP and collaboration with teachers, parents, and students
	8. Participate in transition planning
	9. Develop IEP strategies based on case study results
	10. Provide individual counseling
	11. Provide group counseling
Systems-Level Services	
Domain 5: School-wide practices to promote learning	1. Review district programs (i.e., curriculum, behavior systems, mental health systems)
	2. Participate on teams (e.g., curriculum, positive behavioral interventions and supports [PIS], response to intervention [RtI])
	3. Review school-wide data systems
	4. Create a database of community resources
	5. Interview different professionals in the school
	6. Participate in staff meetings
	7. Conduct benchmarking activities (e.g., CBM assessment)
	8. Analyze school-wide behavior and academic data
	9. Provide small group interventions (e.g., Tier 2)
Domain 6: Preventive and responsive services	1. Review district's crisis plan
	2. Participate on the crisis team
	3. Provide crisis intervention services to students and staff
	4. Maintain an individual counseling caseload
	5. Provide group counseling
	6. Cofacilitate a prevention-oriented student or parent group
	7. Participate in peer mediation
	8. Use behavior management techniques
	9. Participate in child find activities and preschool screenings

(*continued*)

TABLE 5.1 Suggested Practicum Activities (*continued*)

NASP Practice Domain	Suggested Practicum Activities
Domain 7: Family–school collaboration services	1. Attend meetings and become involved with parent groups 2. Provide ongoing home and school communication 3. Research referrals process for community agencies and facilities 4. Review procedures for obtaining and sending information about children 5. Become familiar with state and federal services 6. Develop a resource directory for parents

Foundations of School Psychological Service Delivery

Domain 8: Diversity in development and learning	1. Review relevant literature 2. Work with teachers, parents, and students of diverse backgrounds 3. Participate in team meetings regarding least restrictive educational environment 4. Examine the potential influence of social, cultural, and economic factors in district 5. Use culturally competent approach in assessment 6. Use culturally competent approach while developing interventions or IEP 7. Consider linguistic factors in assessment and intervention activities 8. Conduct nonbiased assessments 9. Choose assessments that consider a student's primary and secondary language 10. Develop interventions that reflect understanding of potential influences
Domain 9: Research and program evaluation	1. Use single case design to evaluate student outcomes 2. Review literature on specific topics 3. Participate in ongoing research or evaluation studies 4. Develop evidence base for intervention strategies 5. Conduct program evaluation of new or existing district programs 6. Conduct needs assessment for staff or parents 7. Conduct survey research on important district initiatives
Domain 10: Legal, ethical, and professional practice	1. Practice in accordance with the NASP principles for professional ethics 2. Review laws related to special education programming 3. Review laws for general education programming and service delivery 4. Practice in accordance with federal and state laws 5. Hold membership with professional organizations 6. Attend and participate in meetings and conventions 7. Keep logs and appropriate counseling notes

Supervisors should also consider both the unique characteristics of the practicum site, as well as individual supervisee interests, strengths, and abilities when helping trainees explore new roles and responsibilities. The primary roles of any particular school psychologist may vary greatly depending on supervisor training and skills, as well as individual district needs. For example, a supervisor working in an elementary school setting may spend a great deal of time engaged in activities related to district RtI implementation, while a supervisor employed in a high school setting may be responsible for conducting a variety of counseling groups each year. Supervisors working in districts that employ multiple school psychologists may also have specific individual assignments (e.g., response-to-intervention [RtI] coach, assessment team, mental health) within the district. Supervisees also come with a set of requirements from their training institution (e.g., assignments, hour requirements, area of focus) and individual interests in the field (e.g., experience with particular populations, roles). Thus, it is not uncommon for supervisors and supervisees to struggle, at times, with a mismatch in the alignment between district opportunities for training and trainee requirements, goals, and expectations. We have developed the practicum activity worksheet to assist supervisors in identifying practicum activities that can be appropriately addressed in the site and also align with trainee goals (see Handout 5.1).

GAINING INDEPENDENCE

Supervisees who are actively involved in their own professional development by advocating for their training needs are often viewed positively by supervisors and other school personnel. They are commonly referred to as candidates who "take initiative" or are "self-starters" and are often viewed as valuable assets to many school teams. We think all of these terms that supervisors use to describe some candidates are related to what Newman (2013) describes as the "proactive intern," a trainee who thinks critically about the field training experience and uses that information to advocate for changes that will enhance his or her learning. While Newman uses this concept to more specifically describe the role of the school psychology *intern*, we feel that training practicum candidates to be proactive in their professional development is an excellent prerequisite for success during more advanced fieldwork. Proactive trainees look for changes to the self or environment that will contribute to professional development by seeking out information, seeking out opportunities, having a proactive attitude, and attending to self-care needs (Newman, 2013). Supervisors can assist trainees in their move to more independence by fostering professional behaviors or "work characteristics" that will promote independence and growth.

Following is a four-step process supervisors can use to identify which types of roles and activities they may assign to supervisees during the practicum. This process may be used at any point during the practicum to help both supervisors and supervisees determine new areas for training.

Step 1: Survey Supervisee Interests

Ask your supervisee to identify three National Association of School Psychologists (NASP) practice domains where he or she would like additional experience. Ask your supervisee to generate a list of three to four activities within each domain that may be of interest. (Note: They can use Table 5.1 as a reference.)

Step 2: Identify Unique Characteristics of Site

Identify a list of five to seven activities that your supervisee has yet to explore and are unique to your site (e.g., participate on crisis team, attend parent group, observe self-contained classroom). These may be activities that you enjoy in your role as a school psychologist or feel it is important for your supervisee to experience before termination of the practicum. Now organize your list of activities into the corresponding NASP practice domains (e.g., attend parent group falls under Domain 7: Family–School Collaboration Services).

Step 3: Collaboratively Generate New List of Activities

Review your lists together and discuss commonalities among the ideas you generated. Identify two practice domains you would like to target and choose up to four activities you will facilitate.

Step 4: Return to Supervisee Interests

Have your supervisee return to his or her list and star two activities that are important to the supervisee and did not make the previous list. It is likely these activities did not make the previous list because they may be difficult to facilitate in your site (i.e., few opportunities, not an area you feel competent supervising). Identify resources you may access to facilitate the activities (e.g., other school personnel, secondary supervisors, partner sites, university faculty). Make an effort to facilitate at least one of the activities, if feasible.

So what professional work characteristics does a more independent practicum supervisee need? For the purposes of this discussion, we will relate this question back to one of the tools we have included in the book. In Appendix A, we present a sample supervisor evaluation tool that may be used to assess trainee skill during the practicum. The final section of this evaluation requires assessment of trainee professional comportment. While there are several important work characteristics assessed in this section, we feel that those most closely related to independence are the following: *reflective practice, accountability for learning, flexibility, enthusiasm,* and *self-awareness.*

We will expand on each of these professional behaviors further. Practicum candidates engage in *reflective practice* when they analyze past experiences to improve future performance. For example, a candidate may learn through early consultation with a teacher that e-mail is not an effective mode of communication and begin to connect with the teacher in person before school to schedule important follow-up meetings to improve the consultation process. Supervisees are *accountable for learning* when they show active engagement in their own professional development and learning. This may include requests for resources and instruction, requests for assistance to solve problems that arise in the field, and use of feedback and supervision to change or improve practice. Practicum candidates demonstrate *flexibility* when they are able to make appropriate adjustments to their professional practice when expectations, roles, or responsibilities change or vary. For example, a supervisee may easily adjust his or her schedule to assess a student after learning of a change in the classroom schedule. Supervisees show *enthusiasm* in fieldwork when they demonstrate a positive attitude and eagerness to engage in professional development. A candidate who is enthusiastic may respond to directives to new assignments by using statements such as "I'm really looking forward to this", "I think I will learn a lot from this experience"; and "Thanks for this opportunity." Alternatively, a candidate who struggles to demonstrate enthusiasm in the field may respond to similar directives by questioning or challenging the supervisor (e.g., "I have already done this" or "Could I do something else?") or looking for ways to avoid the task (e.g., suggesting they do not have the resources or time). Finally, practicum candidates demonstrate *self-awareness* when they can accurately assess their own skills and abilities and understand how these impact their work in the field. For example, a supervisee who is shy and reserved may discuss this with his or her supervisor and ask for strategies that will help the supervisee develop relationships with staff and parents.

Attending to the development of these professional behaviors, in particular, will increase trainee capacity to engage in independent practice. It is important to note that the level of independence during the practicum training will likely be limited to some basic role expansion (e.g., exposure to new roles and activities) and slightly more responsibility in areas of proficiency (e.g., more indirect monitoring of casework). This is unlike training at the internship level, where it is expected that school psychology candidates achieve breadth and depth during their field work.

Promoting trainee independence may also require attention to trainee perceptions and overall mindset about readiness for advancement. One of the new buzz phrases in education today that may be worth paying attention to is the idea of "grit." Grit is a positive, noncognitive personality trait defined as passion for and perseverance toward challenging or long-term goals (Duckworth & Gross, 2014). Grittier teachers have been found to outperform their less gritty colleagues and were less likely to leave their classroom midyear (Roberson-Kraft & Duckworth, 2014). We suggest that supervisors may be able to apply this concept in an effort to develop more resilient school psychologists. One strategy related to grit is what Carol Dweck has termed a "growth mindset"—the belief that success comes from effort. Supervisors can promote a growth mindset by cultivating trainee passion and supporting perseverance when trainees are challenged in the field.

Supervision Strategies to Promote Independence

Supervisors can help to promote supervisee independence by first prompting candidates to self-evaluate their own professional behaviors, such as those we have identified in the previous section. Candidates who can accurately identify their own strengths and weaknesses will be more prepared to plan for their own professional advancement by building on their strengths and identifying supports to address their limitations. One useful activity is for both supervisor and supervisee to evaluate the trainee's professional work characteristics and compare and discuss ratings. Providing supervisees the opportunity to compare ratings with a supervisor will help to build accuracy in their own self-evaluation. Asking supervisees to self-assess their own behavior may also alleviate some of the stress that supervisors may feel about providing feedback on professional dispositions. A trainee may identify a particular personal limitation in his or her own self-assessment (e.g., difficulty with change) that a supervisor was reluctant to address due to fear of upsetting the otherwise pleasant and productive trainee. As a follow-up activity to this assessment, supervisors can direct trainees to use this information to develop goals and a plan for continued professional development. As part of this plan, supervisors should consider both resources and opportunities they may provide in order to support goal achievement. Table 5.2 provides a list of activities that supervisors may use to help promote the professional work characteristics outlined in this chapter.

TABLE 5.2   Activities to Develop Professional Work Characteristics

Professional Work Characteristic	Potential Supervision Activities
Reflective practice	■ Facilitate multiple practice opportunities for various activities ■ Prompt supervisee to use process notes to document and examine work ■ Encourage supervisee to keep a professional journal to examine work ■ De-brief with supervisee after important activities and meetings to examine practice ■ Ask reflective questions during supervision such as "What do you think went well?" or "What might you do differently in the future?"
Accountability for learning	■ Prompt supervisee to identify resources needed when assigned new tasks ■ Make a "post feedback plan" with supervisee to follow-up on how feedback is used to change or maintain practice ■ Assist supervisee to develop long-term goals and short-term objectives ■ Prompt regular review of professional goals and growth (e.g., monthly review) ■ Prompt supervisee to prepare for supervision sessions and be prepared with questions and objectives
Flexibility	■ Prompt supervisee to adjust expectations when situations change ■ Help supervisee explore alternative solutions when situations change ■ Prompt supervisee to "plan ahead" for changes or interruptions to field work ■ Prompt supervisee to allow room in daily and weekly schedule for changes, unexpected requests, or crises
Enthusiasm	■ Model enthusiasm for profession and job expectations ■ Explain purpose and benefits of tasks that are assigned (e.g., how task will enhance practice or development) ■ Ask supervisee to provide feedback on tasks and assignments regularly ■ Help supervisee explore individual interests in the field ■ Encourage supervisee to become involved in professional organizations or work groups
Self-awareness	■ Provide opportunity for self-assessment with rubrics, evaluation tools, and checklists ■ "Compare and share" assessment ratings on occasion to promote supervisee accuracy in self-assessment ■ Prompt supervisee to consider his or her role and effectiveness in certain situations (e.g., "What behaviors do you think were effective/ineffective in that situation?") ■ Prompt supervisee to evaluate self via audio or video recording ■ Encourage supervisee to gather peer feedback regularly

Supervisors can also assist supervisees in becoming more independent by encouraging them to take risks and maintain a healthy perspective about their work in the field. Teaching candidates to create feasible and desirable professional goals can help them do just that! Mental contrasting is a self-regulation strategy used to evaluate the feasibility of one's goals by imagining both a desired future and considering potential obstacles for goal achievement (Oettingen, 2000). In short, mental contrasting can help to decide whether it is worthwhile to commit to a goal or not. This strategy has been shown to be an effective tool for health care professionals in managing the demands of everyday work life (Oettingen, Mayer, & Brinkmann, 2010). Gabriel Oettingen has developed an evidence-based self-regulatory tool called the wish outcome obstacle plan (WOOP). The first three components (wish outcome obstacle) use a visualization strategy to help one gain a better sense of reality by helping to identify wishes and clearly identifying obstacles that stand in the way of these wishes. The final component (plan) of WOOP helps one to prepare and overcome potential obstacles that may interfere with goal attainment. Supervisors can train candidates to use the strategy with the following four simple steps: (a) name a wish that is attainable or realistic for you; (b) take a few minutes to imagine what would happen if that wish came true, allowing the images to flow freely through your mind; (c) identify the main obstacles to attaining the wish and imagine it for a few minutes; and (d) develop a plan for addressing the obstacles by identifying an if–then statement (i.e., if faced with obstacle X, then you will take action Y). There is also a WOOP app for iOS or Android that teaches the strategy and allows one to monitor goals over time.

SELF-CARE

An increase in supervisee independence and additional roles and responsibilities are likely to create new stress in the supervisory relationship. Supervisees may be stressed by the demands of learning new roles, demonstrating skill and proficiency, and taking a more active role in one's own professional development, while supervisors may feel increased anxiety about maintaining client welfare, relinquishing control, and remaining effective as a supervisor. We feel that it is an ideal time to focus on self-care in supervision.

"Stress is an elevation in a person's state of arousal or readiness, caused by some stimulus or demand" (U.S. Department of Health and Human Services, 2005, p. 1). When well-managed, stress is helpful in mobilizing us to get things done and attend to important events (e.g., finish a report for an early deadline, respond to a student crisis, consult with colleagues about a difficult case). When stress becomes extreme or is not managed, however, it can impact both physical and mental health (Bryce, 2001). Increased levels of stress may also lead to occupational burnout (Rosenberg & Pace, 2006), a syndrome that involves depersonalization (e.g., negative, callous, or detached response to others), emotional exhaustion (e.g., feeling drained, lack of energy), and a sense of low personal accomplishment (e.g., feelings of incompetence, lack of productivity; Maslach, 1993).

It is readily recognized that burnout is a problem in helping professions and there is some evidence that school psychologists may be at an increased risk when compared to other mental health professionals (Huebner, 1993). Stress may also impact professional effectiveness and negatively impact client welfare (Barnett, 2008). It is thus a professional responsibility to manage and recognize one's own physical and mental health and, ultimately, readiness for the job. As outlined in the American Psychological Association's (2010) *Ethical Principles of Psychologists and Code of Conduct*, "psychologists strive to be aware of the possible effect of their own physical and mental health on their ability to help those with whom they work" (Principal A, Beneficience and Nonmalficience) and "refrain from initiating an activity when they know or should know that there is a substantial likelihood that their personal problems will prevent them from performing their work-related activities in a competent manner" (2.06, Personal Problems and Conflicts).

Supervision Activities to Support Self-Care

In order to help others, we need to take good care of ourselves. Self-care can be thought of as providing adequate attention to one's own physical and psychological wellness (Beauchamp & Childress, 2001). Busy school psychologists know this may be easier said than done and that self-care can easily fall to the wayside when schedules are hectic and demands are high. Norcross and Barnett (2008) highlight this paradox of self-care quite simply—we often fail at taking care of ourselves at the expense of taking care of others. Few school psychologists would argue that self-care is an important and essential professional disposition to be effective in serving students, families, and schools. Many school psychologists would also likely agree that they have not been adequately trained to consider their own self-care and work in settings that do not foster the practice. We suggest that training per-service school psychologists to incorporate self-care during the practicum may be foundational for professional growth.

Practicum supervisors can support trainee self-care with two key activities: (a) monitoring and modeling their own professional self-care, and (b) encouraging supervisees to develop their own set of self-care strategies. Norcross and Barnett (2008) outline five fundamental lessons about self-care from the literature: (a) focus on finding strategies (e.g., setting boundaries) versus techniques (e.g., 90% rule: Schedule only 90% of your time, allowing 10% for emergencies, personal demands, and self-care); (b) have a variety of self-care strategies versus being well-versed in one; (c) focus on the person-in-environment (e.g., individual limitations and environmental stressors); (d) tailor self-care to the individual practitioner; and (e) embrace self-care in the office and at home. One thing is quite clear from the principles—there is not a "one size fits all" plan for self-care. While supervisors can model the process of developing and following a self-care plan, supervisees will need to design a plan that is unique to their personal interests, stressors, and resources. Perhaps the most important thing to keep in mind is that an effective self-care plan is the one that is used!

Identifying self-care techniques (e.g., yoga, schedules breaks, meditation, professional boundaries, peer networks/support) for an individual plan may prove to be an overwhelming task, as literally thousands exist and have been suggested for use by mental health professionals. In a thoughtful review of the literature, Norcross and Barnett (2008) identified the 12 most effective self-care strategies for psychologists. They are summarized in Table 5.3. The table also provides some suggestions for specific self-care activities relevant to psychologists working in schools. They were developed with consideration of common environmental characteristics of schools and school psychology. Additionally, we have designed a basic self-care checklist that is aligned to the 12 strategies that are highlighted. The checklist can be used as an introductory activity during the initial stages of supervision addressing self-care in the practicum (see Handout 5.2). Both supervisors and supervisees are encouraged to complete the checklist in advance of developing a more formal plan. Lastly, we have included a framework in Handout 5.3 that may be useful in developing a self-care plan. We recommend that both supervisor and supervisee develop plans that will be discussed during supervision and maintained over the school year.

TABLE 5.3 Effective Self-Care Strategies

Self-Care Strategy	General Activities	Field-Specific Activities
Value the person of the professional	■ Assess your own self-care ■ Self-monitor your moods and behavior ■ Get feedback from others ■ Identify effective self-care strategies you already use ■ Prioritize self-care	■ Use a self-care checklist ■ Use a daily mood tracker (e.g., *Moodnotes*) ■ Get feedback from colleagues and loved ones ■ Identify things you do during the school day that promote self-care ■ Identify things you do outside of work that promote self-care ■ Schedule time for self-care

(continued)

TABLE 5.3   Effective Self-Care Strategies (*continued*)

Self-Care Strategy	General Activities	Field-Specific Activities
Refocus on the rewards	■ Identify rewards associated with the profession ■ Feel the career satisfaction	■ Identify your motivation to become a school psychologist ■ Identify the roles and activities that you enjoy most in the field ■ Talk to others about their passion and interest in the field ■ Identify all of the students, families and school staff you have helped over the past few months
Recognize the hazards	■ Recognize the professional hazards that come with the job ■ Share with colleagues ■ Review classic stressors ■ Have self-empathy	■ Identify job stressors: challenging casework, multiple roles, time constraints, size of caseload ■ Start a consultation group with colleagues ■ Give yourself a break! Do not be too hard on yourself if you mess up ■ Appreciate your efforts and personal struggle
Mind the body	■ Protect a healthy sleep schedule ■ Get adequate hydration and nutrition ■ Exercise regularly ■ Get enough physical rest and relaxation	■ Identify a healthy time to go to bed and wake ■ Keep water with you throughout the day ■ Pack snacks for the day ■ Eat lunch in a pleasant setting ■ Take walks outside and around the school often ■ Exercise outside of work ■ Schedule breaks to sit and relax, as necessary ■ Practice relaxation strategies a few minutes each day
Nurture relationships	■ Build a support network at work ■ Develop support outside of work	■ Attend or develop peer support groups ■ Identify 1–2 trusted colleagues ■ Attend social events and gatherings ■ Eat lunch with other colleagues multiple times each week ■ Find a mentor ■ Make time for family and friends ■ Enjoy social groups or activities outside of work

(continued)

TABLE 5.3   Effective Self-Care Strategies (*continued*)

Self-Care Strategy	General Activities	Field-Specific Activities
Set boundaries	■ Maintain boundaries between self and others ■ Maintain boundaries between work and personal life	■ Schedule short breaks during the day ■ Restrict caseload to reasonable limit ■ Limit intense casework ■ Use the 90% rule: schedule only 90% of your time to allow 10% for emergencies, personal demands, and self-care ■ Learn to say "no" when appropriate ■ Leave work at a reasonable time each day ■ Set a limit on how much work is completed outside of the workday ■ Set rules for e-mail and communication outside of work
Restructure cognitions	■ Monitor internal dialogue ■ Maintain healthy expectations for performance	■ Take note of negative thoughts and practice reframing them with a preferred method (e.g., cognitive-behavioral therapy) ■ Practice positive self-talk ■ Discuss expectations with supervisors regularly ■ Consult with peers and colleagues about work expectations
Sustain healthy escapes	■ Identify and practice healthy escapes ■ Monitor use of unhealthy escapes	■ Enjoy a meal with friends and colleagues ■ Read an interesting book ■ Develop a hobby ■ Take time to laugh! ■ Monitor use of alcohol, caffeine, and other unhealthy substances ■ Monitor isolation from others (too much time alone)
Create a flourishing environment	■ Evaluate your work environment with the following dimensions: work load, control, reward, sense of community, respect, and similar values ■ Determine what can be changed ■ Enhance comfort of work environment	■ Change little things that impact satisfaction (e.g., commute with a colleague, join committees with like-minded peers, advocate for easy access to resources, such as test kits, computer, and office supplies) ■ Make your office a comfortable space (e.g., hang pictures, adjust the lighting, add personal furniture) ■ Negotiate when possible (e.g., preferred school assignments, roles/responsibilities, new office space)

(continued)

TABLE 5.3 Effective Self-Care Strategies (*continued*)		
Self-Care Strategy	General Activities	Field-Specific Activities
Undergo personal therapy	■ Seek therapeutic support when necessary ■ Supplement with own self-analysis ■ Engage in other types of self-development (e.g., yoga, meditation, mindfulness)	■ Maintain a personal referral list for therapeutic support and access when necessary ■ Practice journal writing or reflection activities ■ Incorporate mindfulness into your day ■ Take a few minutes to meditate each day (e.g., 5–10 minutes before first school bell)
Cultivate spirituality and mission	■ Revisit your passion for field ■ Connect to spiritual sources ■ Merge your vocation with social activism	■ Develop a personal mission for your work ■ Explore spiritual sources ■ Get involved in professional advocacy efforts
Foster creativity and growth	■ Get involved in diverse professional activities ■ Recognize that self-renewal is an ongoing process ■ Be flexible and adaptable	■ Maintain professional memberships (e.g., National Association of School Psychologists, American Psychological Association, state organizations) ■ Attend professional conferences ■ Join professional councils, boards, or organizations ■ Revisit professional activities every 3 years and look for new opportunities ■ Revisit professional growth and plan annually ■ Set short- and long-term professional goals and monitor annually

EVALUATION OF THE SUPERVISEE

As discussed in earlier chapters, regular monitoring of the supervisee's training plan ensures that practicum activities and goals are proactively addressed throughout the training year. At this stage in the practicum, supervisors should review the training plan to evaluate the candidate's level of experience in various school psychological roles. Some supervisors may find it helpful to consult a copy of the National Association of School Psychologists (NASP) practice domains as part of this evaluation. Supervisors may consider using Table 5.1 as a tool for exploring ways to facilitate new activities that will help each individual candidate gain experience in domains that are under represented.

Directions: Place a check mark next to all of the activities you already use for regular self-care.

Self-Care Activities	☑
Value the Person of the Professional	
Assess your own self-care	
Self-monitor your moods and behavior	
Get feedback from others	
Identify effective self-care strategies you already use	
Prioritize self-care	
Refocus on the Rewards	
Identify rewards associated with profession	
Feel career satisfaction	
Recognize the Hazards	
Recognize professional hazards that come with your job	
Share job stressors and concerns with colleagues	
Have identified the classic stressors associated with your job	
Have self-empathy	
Mind the Body	
Protect a healthy sleep schedule	
Get adequate hydration and nutrition	
Exercise regularly	
Get enough physical rest and relaxation	
Nurture Relationships	
Have a support network	
Have support outside of work	
Set Boundaries	
Maintain boundaries between self and others	
Maintain boundaries between work and personal life	
Restructure Cognitions	
Monitor internal dialogue	
Maintain healthy expectations for performance	

(continued)

HANDOUT 5.2   Self-Care Checklist (*continued*)

Self-Care Activities	☑
Sustain Healthy Escapes	
Identify and practice healthy escapes	
Monitor use of unhealthy escapes	
Create a Flourishing Environment	
Evaluate your work environment with the following dimensions: work load, control, reward, sense of community, respect, and similar values	
Determine what can be changed	
Enhance comfort of work environment	
Undergo Personal Therapy	
Seek therapeutic support when necessary	
Supplement with own self-analysis	
Engage in other types of self-development (e.g., yoga, meditation, mindfulness)	
Cultivate Spirituality and Mission	
Revisit your passion for the field	
Connect to spiritual sources	
Merge your vocation with social activism	
Foster Creativity and Growth	
Get involved in diverse professional activities	
Recognize that self-renewal is an ongoing process	
Be flexible and adaptable	

Directions: Consider what you do now for self-care and list those activities in Section 1 of this worksheet. Next, identify any strategies that you will begin to incorporate as part of your self-care plan (Section 2). Pay close attention to domains that you have not been addressing in the past. In Section 3, identify barriers that might interfere with your plan and how you will address them.

Section 1: Identify current self-care strategies that you currently use and are working well. *Note:* Review areas that you checked on your self-assessment.

Section 2: Identify one or two new strategies that you will begin to incorporate as part of your self-care plan. *Note:* Review those areas that were not checked on your self-assessment and star areas that you think will work well for you.

Strategy #1:

Strategy #2:

(continued)

HANDOUT 5.3   Self-Care Plan Worksheet (*continued*)

Section 3: Provide a summary of your new self-care plan and prepare for potential challenges in implementing it successfully. List all of the self-care strategies you would like to use in column one, identify potential barriers to using the strategies in column two, and identify strategies for overcoming these barriers in column three.

List of Current and New Self-Care Strategies	Potential Barriers	How I Will Address Barriers

Supervisors should also consider careful evaluation of each candidate's professional work characteristics and self-care practices during this stage of training. It may be particularly helpful for both university and site supervisors to conduct this evaluation together with the candidate. This could be accomplished through a site visit or with a more formal evaluation tool. Regardless of the format, it is an excellent time to provide the candidate both verbal and written feedback regarding his or her progress in the development of important professional behaviors.

SUPERVISOR TO-DO LIST

☐ Use less direct supervision and assign more advanced casework in areas where supervisee has demonstrated competence
☐ Facilitate new activities in practice domains where supervisee has not gained experience
☐ Prompt supervisee to conduct self-assessment of professional work characteristics
☐ Help the supervisee develop realistic expectations for practice by developing attainable professional goals
☐ Take time to develop your own self-care plan
☐ Assist the supervisee in developing a personal self-care plan

REFERENCES

American Psychological Association. (2010). *Ethical principles of psychologists and code of conduct*. Washington, DC: Author.

Barnett, J. E. (2008). Impaired professionals: Distress, professional impairment, self-care, and psychological wellness. In M. Hersen & A. M. Gross (Eds.), *Handbook of clinical psychology* (Vol. 1, pp. 857–884). Hoboken, NJ: Wiley and Sons.

Beauchamp, T. L., & Childress, J. F. (2001). *Principles of biomedical ethics* (5th ed.). New York, NY: Oxford University Press.

Bryce, C. P. (2001). *Stress management in disasters*. Washington, DC: Pan American Health Organization.

Castillo, J. M., Curtis, J. M., & Gelley, C. (2012). School psychology 2010—Part 2: School psychologists' professional practices and implications for the field. *Communiqué*, *40*(8), 4–6.

Duckworth, A., & Gross, J. J. (2014). *Self-control and grit: Related but separable determinants of success. Current Directions in Psychological Science*. New York, NY: Sage. doi:10.1177/0963721414541462

Huebner, E. S. (1993). Burnout among school psychologists in the USA: Further data related to its prevalence and correlates. *School Psychology International*, *14*(2), 99–109.

Maslach, C. (1993). Burnout: A multidimensional perspective. In W. B. Schaufeli, C. Maslach, & T. Marek (Eds.), *Professional burnout: Recent developments in theory and research* (pp. 19–32). Washington, DC: Taylor & Francis.

National Association of School Psychologists. (2010). *Model for comprehensive and integrated school psychological services*. Bethesda, MD: Author.

Newman, D. (2013). *Demystifying the school psychology internship: A dynamic guide for interns and supervisors*. New York, NY: Routledge.

Norcross, J. C., & Barnett, J. E. (2008). Self-care as ethical imperative. *The Register Report*, *34*, 20–27. Retrieved from http://www.nationalregister.org/trr_spring08_norcross.html

Oettingen, G. (2000). Expectancy effects on behavior depend on self-regulatory thought. *Social Cognition*, *18*(2), 101–129.

Oettingen, G., Mayer, D., & Brinkmann, B. (2010). Mental contrasting of future and reality: Managing the demands of everyday life in health care professionals. *Journal of Personnel Psychology*, *9*(3), 138–144.

Roberson-Kraft, C., & Duckworth, A. (2014). True grit: Trait-level perseverance and passion for long-term goals predicts effectiveness and retention among novice teachers. *Teachers College Record*, *116*(030302), 1–27.

Rosenberg, T., & Pace, M. (2006). Burnout among mental health professionals: Special considerations for the marriage and family therapist. *Journal of Marital and Family Therapy*, *32*(1), 87–99.

U.S. Department of Health and Human Services. (2005). *A guide to managing stress in crisis response professions*. Washington, DC: Author.

SIX

PLANNING FOR INTERNSHIP

School psychology practica help prepare candidates for internship, the capstone field experience in training. While there is a somewhat vague direction from the National Association of School Psychologists (NASP) and the American Psychological Association (APA) for practicum training, the requirements for internship are quite clear and create consistency across training programs nationally. The main purpose of the internship is to offer school psychology candidates the opportunity to integrate and apply professional knowledge and skills acquired in program coursework and practica (NASP, 2010). Unlike practica, which are most typically arranged by university faculty and are unpaid training experiences, internships serve as the first training opportunity where candidates are actively involved in the process of securing a formal field training position.

Candidates should feel prepared for the internship and supervisors should feel comfortable endorsing candidates' advancement to the internship by the end of the practicum experience. Supervisors and supervisees, thus, should begin planning for the transition to the internship in advance of the termination of the practicum training. We find that a good time to begin this process is right before the midyear mark of a 9-month practicum, around December of a typical academic year. This chapter explores various supervision activities related to the process of internship preparation and includes: (a) a review of the requirements for the internship in school psychology, (b) a discussion of how to promote professional development consistent with these requirements, (c) a review of the use of portfolios during training, and (d) an evaluation of supervisee readiness for advancement.

REQUIREMENTS FOR THE INTERNSHIP

School psychology candidates are bound by the requirements of their training institution, which are bound, at a minimum, by their state accrediting bodies (e.g., state board of education) and often by professional accrediting bodies (e.g., NASP, APA). While the requirements for internship across each of these bodies often align, even the smallest nuanced difference can cause a trainee difficulty in degree completion or becoming credentialed in the field. Novice trainees require a great deal of professional mentoring in understanding the requirements of the internship and how specific training experiences may best align to their long-term professional goals. We provide a brief overview of the requirements documented in the NASP (2010) *Standards for Graduate Preparation of School Psychologists.*

The school psychology internship is a supervised, culminating, comprehensive field experience that is completed for credit and prior to the awarding of the specialist or doctoral degree (NASP, 2010). School psychology candidates demonstrate readiness for the internship when they have successfully completed all coursework in the training program, completed all relevant practica, and passed all other training program benchmarks (e.g., state licensure exams, comprehensive examinations). Perhaps, with the exception of the dissertation defense at the doctoral level of training, it should be expected that candidates have completed all other program requirements before beginning the internship. The primary purpose for the internship is to provide the candidate breadth and depth of training in all of the domains of school psychology (NASP, 2010) with an end goal of having the candidate ready to practice as an entry-level school psychologist upon completion of field training. While this is not an exhaustive list of requirements, the following are key elements of the field experience: (a) the internship is completed for a minimum of 1 academic year and 1,200 (specialist)/1,500 (doctoral) hours, with at least 600 hours in a school setting; (b) supervision is provided by a credentialed school psychologist for an average of at least 2 hours in face-to-face supervision each week; (c) there is clear collaboration between the training institution and field site in the documentation and evaluation of the candidate's training (e.g., training agreement, formal evaluation forms); and (d) there is systematic evaluation of the candidate's readiness for the field, as evidenced by direct, measurable, positive impact on children, families, schools, and other consumers (NASP, 2010). With these requirements in mind, practicum supervisors are preparing trainees to have the knowledge, skills, and professional dispositions necessary to engage in a full-time field experience covering the full range of practice domains, with the expectation that they will demonstrate effective practice as measured by the impact on the clients they serve.

Although training programs must approve the internship field site, school psychology candidates must apply for and secure their own internship placements. Most trainees will secure paid employment positions with a school district or agency, such as a clinic, and be required to navigate all of the employee procedures, policies, and activities in addition to university processes. Supervisors can assist practicum candidates by understanding the expectations of the professional world and help them understand how they relate to their overall training experience. For example, the amount of compensation, policies related to leave and sick days, and general resources (e.g., office space, computer) available to employees may greatly impact trainee satisfaction during the internship. In addition, it is important for practicum candidates to ask about how supervision is structured during the internship, including amount, formats, and personnel providing the supervision.

Supervision Activities for Internship Preparation

Supervisors can help to prepare candidates for the internship by orienting them to important training requirements, providing mentorship in activities related to securing a site, and helping them develop a network of professional resources. To begin, supervisors should assist trainees in understanding the requirements of their training institution, state, and other relevant credentialing bodies (e.g., NASP, APA). University supervisors can provide this orientation via well-documented internship manuals and professional meetings or presentations for students. Field supervisors could encourage trainees to develop a personal "cheat sheet" by closely reviewing their university training documents and state and national requirements for credentialing as an exercise in orientation.

Securing an internship may be the first time some practicum candidates have ever had to seek employment in a professional setting. Many will need guidance in how to search for positions, prepare application materials, and to conduct themselves during an interview. Supervisors can provide trainees with support in the search process by both orienting them to resources (e.g., job boards, career sites) for finding open positions and helping them narrow the search to positions that will be a good fit for their skills and professional goals. University supervisors may be particularly helpful in the search process by conducing outreach to potential sites and compiling a list or database of sites that are seeking interns. One of the authors collaborates each year with faculty from other school psychology programs in her state to gather this information via a *Survey Monkey* questionnaire that is sent to supervisors from all former internship sites. The results can be accessed via a database that is available to all interns in the state and is updated throughout the year as sites provide their information.

The novice candidate may be eager to submit applications to a vast number of positions without considering the fit of the site to their professional goals and personal strengths and experiences. Supervisors should caution trainees to apply largely to positions that align with their training goals and are of considerable interest to the candidate. Suggesting that candidates apply to their top three to five positions in an original search may be a good rule of thumb.

Supervisors can also assist in trainee preparation of important application materials, such as letters of recommendation, cover letters, essays, and the development of a curriculum vita or resume. Perhaps the best way to help is to direct the supervisee to the university career services center or other helpful resources such as Otis and Pincus's (n.d.) clinical internship guide. It is also helpful to provide the trainee suggested timelines for the preparation of these materials so that they are adequately prepared for the search process and ready to apply for competitive positions. A sample timeline for a specialist-level intern candidate is provided in Box 6.1. The timelines and activities may vary slightly depending on where the candidate is training (e.g., state and institution). Also, doctoral-level interns are likely to consider obtaining an APA-approved internship site and would follow timelines and activities associated with the Association of Psychology Postdoctoral and Internship Centers (APPIC).

A strong application will help a trainee get an interview, but a strong interview will secure a position! Preparing school psychology candidates for the demands of an interview is critical to helping them achieve their professional goals. At a minimum, supervisors can provide a list of sample interview questions in preparation for the interview. Even better, supervisors can provide the trainee practice by facilitating mock interview situations. Field supervisors have the unique advantage of closely simulating a real interview by inviting teachers, administrators, and other school personnel to ask the supervisee questions. University supervisors may consider inviting program faculty, advanced students, or other professionals to role-play with intern candidates. Regardless of the format, focus should be on providing

---

BOX 6.1 Sample Specialist-Level Internship Timeline

To Do	Due Date
Prepare internship materials and research sites	December–January
Attend state convention and job fair	February
Begin actively applying for positions	February
State internship acceptance date	March 15th
Take state content exam (must pass before start of internship)	April–July
Submit university and district paperwork and documentation	April–August

the trainee with exposure to the experience of the interview and feedback on performance. There are also some excellent web-based resources that candidates can use to help perfect their interview as well. Practicum candidates from one of the author's training institutions have access to a resource called *InterviewStream* via the school's career services website. It is an incredibly helpful video interviewing platform that allows candidates to practice interviews at their own pace and offers feedback on performance.

The internship search can be a stressful process for the practicum candidate. Candidates are most likely balancing the search process with the completion of university coursework and practicum. Supervisors can help to alleviate some of this stress by providing supervisees with opportunities to network with their peers and mentors in the field. Connecting candidates to former interns and program alumni via a panel presentation or social event can be a helpful way to offer support, as trainees often find it useful to connect with those that have very recent and similar experiences to their own. This mentorship could be easily facilitated through active student groups, such as the School Psychology Student Organization (SPSO) in a university. One of the authors collaborates with program faculty from other regional school psychology programs to host an annual student "Intern Event" each year. The event offers candidates an opportunity to prepare for the internship placement process by visiting with supervisors from potential sites, participating in a question-and-answer session with current interns, attending a presentation on licensure, and participating in other relevant application and interview activities (e.g., CV prep, mock interviews). Both candidates and site supervisors appreciate this event each year. Supervisors should also encourage supervisees to consider how they may network by having a thoughtful digital presence. Professional sites such as LinkedIn offer candidates yet another avenue to connect with peers and potential employers for support, information, and resources.

TRAINEE PROFESSIONAL DEVELOPMENT

Planning for internship is a natural professional transition for the school psychology candidate and serves as a great time for trainees to reflect upon what they have accomplished, what they still need to learn, and how they will get the skills they need in order to achieve their own professional goals. We think that supervisors can assist trainees in these activities by teaching trainees to engage in reflective practice, meaningful self-assessment, and professional goal development. Each of these is discussed in further detail in this section.

Reflective Practice

A "reflective practitioner" is described as one who uses reflection as a tool for examining an experience to learn from it and solve complex problems of professional practice (Schon, 1983). Practitioners who engage in reflective practice do so with the deliberate intention of examining past experiences in order to learn from them and create new knowledge that will guide future practice. It has been suggested that by encouraging practitioners to reflect upon practice, they will have opportunity to explore good practice, identify areas of improvement, and formulate ideas for change (Knowles, Gilbourne, Borrie, & Nevill, 2001). In a systematic review of reflective practice used in the health professions, Mann, Gordon, and MacLeod (2009) found the following common elements of reflective practice: (a) past experience informs planning, (b) it is promoted by appropriate supervision, and (c) it occurs most often in novel or challenging situations. Thus, we recommend that supervisors create a system for trainee self-reflection whereby trainees engage in reflective activities when they come across challenges in their field work. For the practicum candidate, this is perhaps most likely to occur when classroom-based theory is not easily translated into site-based practice. Used in this way, reflection is viewed as a learning strategy that assists trainees in connecting new experiences during practice to existing knowledge and skills gained through previous training.

Supervision activities to support reflective practice

Supervisors can prompt supervisee self-reflection through a variety of activities, such as journal writing, the use of thought-provoking questions or "thinking prompts," and discussion about challenging experiences during supervision. Boud's (2001) model for journal writing may be particularly helpful in enhancing the novice practicum candidate's reflective practice, as it includes three occasions for reflection: (a) in anticipation of events, (b) in the midst of action, and (c) after events. Reflection that occurs *in anticipation of events* can help prepare one for an upcoming event by attending to what the learner brings to the situation (e.g., current skills, expectations), the context (e.g., environmental variables), and opportunities for learning and skill development. Reflection *in the midst of action* requires noticing (i.e., having awareness of what is happening around us), intervening (i.e., paying attention to the actions we take), and reflection-in-action (i.e., interpretation of the events and our actions). Reflection *after events* includes a return to the experience, attention to the feelings and emotions experienced during the event, and a reevaluation of the experience. Supervisors may suggest that trainees engage in journal writing in one or all of these stages at various times throughout the practicum training, but we suggest that it may be a particularly useful activity to use during planning and in preparation for the internship. Handout 6.1 provides questions and writing prompts that can be used to engage in Boud's (2001) three stages of journal reflection.

Supervisors may also encourage trainees to engage in reflective practice during individual supervision sessions by prompting them with specific questions or topics for reflection. Johns (2015) developed a model of structured reflection for nurse practitioners with an aim at improving practice and patient outcomes. We think this model is easily adapted to and meaningful to the work of school psychologists as well. Johns's (2015) model includes five cue questions in the following areas: (a) description of the experience (What happened?), (b) reflection (What was I trying to achieve and what are the consequence?), (c) influencing factors (What affected my decision making?), (d) other approaches (What other choices did I have and what are the outcomes associated with those choices?), and (e) learning (How has this experience changed my way of knowing?). Supervisors can incorporate the use of these question prompts regularly during individual sessions to encourage candidates to practice reflective thinking and also help trainees overcome challenging experiences during field training. Practicum candidates who learn these strategies during early field experiences will be better equipped to use them during more advanced field training, such as the internship.

Self-Assessment

Reflection is an important component of self-assessment (Koutsoupidou, 2010), a skill that can help trainees to examine their work and identify professional strengths and weaknesses. "Self-assessment is a process of formative assessment during which students reflect on the quality of their work, judge the degree to which it reflects explicitly stated goals or criteria, and revise accordingly" (Andrade & Valtcheva, 2009, p. 13). When thinking about their readiness for internship training, practicum candidates should take time to thoughtfully consider their own progress toward training expectations. Supervisors can encourage trainee self-assessment with a three-step process: (a) articulate performance expectations, (b) prompt trainee self-assessment, and (c) assist the trainee to revise his or her work through goal setting.

Self-assessment can be a powerful tool, especially when it is used in connection with supervisor feedback. Some supervisors may find that prompting trainees to self-assess their own abilities will help to alleviate some of the discomfort and stress associated with evaluation and feedback activities. Self-assessment is enhanced when students clearly understand the performance criteria (e.g., the trainee is familiar with language and terms

HANDOUT 6.1   Reflective-Practice Activity: Journal Writing

Reflection in Anticipation of Events

This type of reflection can help prepare you for an upcoming event by attending to what you bring to the situation. You should focus on what you can do to make the most of future events.

Learner Characteristics:

1. What skills and abilities will help you in the situation?
2. What are your limitations and how might they impact the situation?
3. What are your intentions and goals for the situation?
4. What are your expectations for the event and the outcomes?

Context:

1. What is the context of the event?
2. How do people relevant to the situation view the event?
3. What are the features of the event that cannot be altered?

Learning Skills and Strategies:

1. What skills might we still need in order to be successful in the event?
2. What learning opportunities or professional development is available?
3. What might I practice before I enter the event?

Reflection in the Midst of Action

This type of reflection requires that you notice (i.e., have awareness of what is happening around you), intervene (i.e., pay attention to the actions you take), and reflect-in-action (i.e., interpret the events and your actions).

Noticing:

1. What do you notice about what is happening around you?
2. What are your thoughts and feelings about what is happening around you?

(continued)

Intervening:
1. What actions are you taking to change or direct the situation?
2. How do your feelings and thoughts impact the situation and your actions?

Reflection-in-Action:
1. What are my interpretations of the events that have occurred?
2. How have my actions to change or direct the situation worked out?

Reflection After Events
This type of reflection includes a return to the experience, attention to the feelings and emotions experienced during the event, and a reevaluation of the experience.

Return to Experience:
1. Provide a full account of what occurred.

Attention to Feelings:
1. How did I feel about the events as they occurred?
2. How do I feel about the events now?

Reevaluation of Experience:
1. How does this experience fit with my previous knowledge and learning?
2. What did I learn from the experience?
3. How does this event impact my future practice?

in evaluation tools), receive instruction or are allowed practice using the performance criteria (e.g., review, model, or request that trainee practices using evaluation tools), feedback is provided on self-assessment, and goals are developed based on the data (Ross, 2006).

Supervision activities to support self-assessment

We feel there are specific activities that are best suited to supervision of the school psychology practicum candidate and these include portfolio assessment, the use of rubrics in evaluation, focus on goal-setting, and explicit instruction in time management. The use of portfolios and goal development is covered in subsequent sections of this chapter, so we focus our discussion here on the use of rubrics in evaluation and instruction in time management.

Rubrics can be used to both teach and evaluate. Supervisors can construct rubrics to teach trainees what is expected of them in the field setting by indicating which skills should be demonstrated and by identifying varying levels of quality associated with each. Appendix D provides an example rubric constructed for use in evaluation of psychoeducational reports submitted via a university practicum seminar. To encourage candidate self-assessment, the university seminar instructor could include this rubric in the seminar syllabus, review it thoroughly during instruction, and request that candidates complete a self-assessment of each report before submitting to the course instructor. During the evaluation period, the university instructor can then provide valuable feedback regarding both candidate performance and accuracy in perception of individual skill. Continued practice with this rubric, and overall self-assessment in general, will hopefully improve candidate self-awareness about abilities and training needs.

Learning to manage one's time as a school psychologist is an invaluable and critical skill in a profession that requires one to juggle multiple roles and schedules in a busy school setting. Practicum candidates can benefit greatly from explicit instruction and modeling from supervisors about how to manage their time so that they meet important deadlines and improve efficiency in their work. Supervisors can do this by orienting trainees to the systems that they use to manage their own time as professionals, such as introducing candidates to the use of common calendar systems (e.g., Microsoft Outlook), district procedures for meeting schedules (e.g., initial and triennial evaluation timelines), and document sharing applications (e.g., Google Docs, Dropbox). We have witnessed supervisors use Google Docs very successfully by creating a shared calendar with trainees so that they have direct oversight of planning and scheduling. Other supervisors may decide to use individual supervision time to review candidate schedules and activities. Regardless of the format, it is important to focus on the foundations of time management during the practicum training, as both independence and workload increase quickly during the internship year. Candidates who do not have strong time-management skills can easily fall behind during an advanced level of field training.

Professional Goal Development

The development and management of professional goals have been a constant theme in this book, as we feel that goals are a guiding force in trainee advancement and growth. In Chapter 1, we recommend that trainees identify initial goals for the practicum experience that are based on personal interests, abilities, and program requirements. In Chapter 5, we suggest that trainees formally revisit their training plan and original goals to help identify new directions for professional growth and advancement. In this chapter, we suggest that trainees consider progress or attainment of their goals for the practicum training and begin to plan ahead for goals that will guide their training during the internship year.

Supervision activities to support professional goal development

The transition from the school psychology practicum to internship requires a great deal of candidate independence and self-awareness in terms of professional development. Candidates will need to evaluate the types of placements that are best suited to their strengths and interests, and consider any challenges they may face in obtaining an internship of choice. Teaching trainees how to develop long-term goals for professional development is a great way to provide direction in preparation for the internship. Supervisors can encourage trainees to think beyond their graduate training and consider how they view themselves as a professional school psychologist. *Where will they work and live? What are their roles and responsibilities as a school psychologist?* Helping trainees develop clear long-term career goals that fit well into their personal lives can help provide direction, increase motivation, and improve planning for professional growth. An activity to assist in long-term goal planning is included in Handout 6.2. Supervisors can encourage trainees to use this worksheet to assist in discussion about career planning and professional growth.

DEVELOPING A PORTFOLIO OF WORK

There has been an increased emphasis on performance-based assessment in the preparation and training of educators, including accreditation and credentialing (Waldron & Prus, 2006), as well as in the hiring, retention, evaluation, and promotion processes of educators in the field (Green & Smyser, 1995). In fact,

HANDOUT 6.2   Long-Term Goal-Setting Activity

STEP 1: Think about where you want to be in 5 years. Ask yourself the following questions: (a) In what type of setting will I work? (b) What will be my roles and responsibilities as a school psychologist? and (c) Where will I live?

STEP 2: Now write down two to three long-term career goals. Next to each goal identify any skills and strengths you have that will help you reach this goal. Also identify any challenges (e.g., weakness or other barriers) that may make achieving each goal difficult. Evaluate each goal, your strengths, and challenges and identify one goal that you would like to work toward achieving.

Long-Term Career Goal	Skills and Strengths	Challenges and Barriers

STEP 3: Write this goal so that it is well-defined and measurable. You can use the *specific, measurable, attainable, realistic,* and *time-bound* (SMART) method.

STEP 4: Break your long-term goal into smaller tasks or chunks that can be accomplished in 6 to 12 months each. Consider the types of professional development or experiences you might need in order to achieve the long-term goal when developing your short-term objectives.

NASP has a national certification system that has a performance-based component and training standards that include requirements for program assessment and accountability. School psychologists interested in obtaining the National Certification in School Psychology (NCSP) are required to either have graduated from a NASP-approved program or to present a portfolio demonstrating attainment of knowledge and skills consistent with the NASP domains of professional practice. Today's school psychology candidates are thus required to demonstrate both what they know and what they are able to do (Waldron & Prus, 2006). Some candidates will be required to demonstrate competence in professional practice domains through portfolio assessment in their training program, while others may simply find it helpful to organize a professional portfolio independent of their training requirements. Practicum supervisors can assist candidates in portfolio development by helping trainees identify authentic products from their field work that showcase specific professional skills and experiences.

Portfolio assessment is a purposeful collection of student work that illustrates efforts, growth, and successes in multiple areas (Arter & Spandel, 1992). Portfolios can be used to document competence, for self-assessment, to plan for professional development, and to evaluate training program preparation. School psychology program portfolios most commonly include the following types of work products: practica products/cases; internship products/cases; course-related products; field site/internship supervisor evaluations; self-reflection statements; research projects; and curriculum vitae or resumes (Waldron & Prus, 2006). Moreover, Waldron and Prus (2006) suggest that specific professional competencies are often addressed through work products from practica and internships, including assessment, consultation, behavior analysis/intervention, counseling, research, training/in-service, prevention, and supervision.

Supervision Activities for Portfolio Development

School psychology candidates will generate several useful products during practicum training that may be an excellent fit for a portfolio of work. Making decisions about which products to include may be difficult for the novice trainee and practicum supervisors are in an ideal position to provide mentoring around these activities. Offering trainees a set of guidelines or inclusion criteria can be incredibly useful in helping them to first begin to organize their work. Salend (2001) identified seven questions that can help candidate's decide what should be included in a professional portfolio of work. We have modified these questions slightly to more specifically address a school psychology portfolio. They are included in Box 6.2.

BOX 6.2 Questions to Guide Product Inclusion in the Portfolio

1. What does the item reveal about my skills, knowledge, experiences, and attitudes?
2. Is the item consistent with my educational philosophy and best practices?
3. Does the item demonstrate my best work?
4. Is the item free of grammatical and other errors?
5. Is the item authentic and showcase my skills and experiences in working with students, families, and other professionals?
6. What competencies and experiences did I engage in to produce this item?
7. What does the item reveal about me on a personal level?

Candidates should be encouraged to revise original work products to reflect "best practices" in the field when including them in the portfolio. This may mean that the candidate makes revisions and changes to original work based on feedback from field supervisors or faculty in the training program. Integrating the feedback is an excellent way to showcase growth and professional reflection. Also, supervisors should discuss the importance of maintaining client confidentiality and the process for obtaining the appropriate permissions to use specific documents in the portfolio. For example, a candidate developing an electronic portfolio may have interest in including a video sample of a teacher consultation and needs to obtain consent from the teacher before sharing this work. It may be helpful to schedule regular supervision time (e.g., once per month) for addressing portfolio development. Supervisors can ask that trainees answer all seven questions in Box 6.2 before introducing a new work product during supervision so that the trainee has engaged in adequate self-reflection about his or her work and its relevance to professional development.

EVALUATION OF THE SUPERVISEE

Supervisors are responsible for determining candidate advancement in the field and ultimately serve as gatekeepers for the profession. Advancement is a high-stakes decision both in terms of the candidate's own professional potential and the welfare of clients served in school settings, making it an incredibly difficult task. Having the right mind-set is the first step in making this decision. "To overcome discomfort about evaluating supervisees, supervisors should consider it an opportunity to provide information and professional development—with the ultimate goals of both protecting students and helping supervisees improve" (Harvey & Struzziero, 2008, p. 408). While advancement decisions will most likely be made during the final summative evaluation of candidates' training, we recommend that supervisors begin to prepare for this activity in the final few months of the practicum.

Adequate preparation can help to alleviate the anxiety and uncertainty that both supervisors and supervisees may experience in the process of evaluation. We suggest that supervisors take time to review with supervisees the university evaluation tools and requirements, as well as any state and national requirements for practice, in preparation for the final evaluation. At this stage in the training, discussion about readiness for advancement should largely be about ensuring that the supervisee is on target to meet all of the requirements and training goals and less on active planning and remediation, if it is necessary. These activities were the focus of previous chapters and should be addressed earlier in the training sequence.

SUPERVISOR TO-DO LIST

☐ Prompt trainee to review requirements for the internship
☐ Assist trainee in securing an internship site aligned to training goals and strengths
☐ Help trainee develop a professional network and support system for internship planning
☐ Promote reflective practice through journal writing and the use of discussion prompts during individual supervision
☐ Promote supervisee self-assessment through portfolio assessment, rubrics, goal-setting, and time management activities
☐ Assist supervisee with career planning through development of long-term goals

REFERENCES

Andrade, H., & Valtcheva, A. (2009). Promoting learning and achievement through self-assessment. *Theory Into Practice*, 48(1), 12–19.

Arter, J. A., & Spandel, V. (1992). Using portfolios of student work in instruction and assessment. *Educational Measurement: Issues and Practice*, 11(1), 36–44.

Boud, D. (2001). Using journal writing to enhance reflective practice. *New Directions in Adult and Continuing Education*, 90, 9–18.

Green, J. E. & Smyser, S. O. (1995). Changing conceptions about teaching: The use of portfolios with pre-service teachers. *Teacher Education Quarterly*, 22, 43–53.

Harvey, V. S., & Struzziero, J. A. (2008). *Professional development and supervision of school psychologists: From intern to expert* (2nd ed.). Thousand Oaks, CA: Corwin Press and National Association of School Psychologists.

Johns, C. (2015). *Becoming a reflective practitioner* (3rd ed.). Hoboken, NJ: Wiley.

Knowles, Z., Gilbourne, D., Borrie, A., & Nevill, A. (2001). Developing the reflective sports coach: A study exploring the processes of reflective practice within a higher education coaching program. *Reflective Practice, 2,* 185–207.

Koutsoupidou, T. (2010). Self-assessment in generalist pre-service kindergarten teachers' education: Insights training, ability, environments, and policies. *Arts Education Policy Review, 111*(3), 105–111.

Mann, K., Gordon, J., & MacLeod, A. (2009). Reflection and reflective practice in health professions education: A systematic review. *Advances in Health Sciences Education, 14*(4), 595–621.

National Association of School Psychologists. (2010). *Standards for the graduate preparation of school psychologists.* Bethesda, MD: Author.

Otis, J. D., & Pincus, D. B. (n.d.). *The clinical psychology internship guide: The primary resource for obtaining your first choice.* Retrieved from http://www.psychzone.com/Intern_Guide.htm

Ross, J. A. (2006). The reliability, validity, and utility of self-assessment. *Practical Assessment Research and Evaluation, 11*(10). Available at http://pareonline.net/getvn.asp?v=11&n=10

Salend, S. J. (2001). Creating your own professional portfolio. *Intervention in School and Clinic, 36*(4), 195–201.

Schon, D. A. (1983). *The reflective practitioner: How professionals think in action.* New York, NY: Basic Books.

Waldron, N., & Prus, J., (2006). *A guide for performance-based assessment, accountability, and program development in school psychology training programs.* Bethesda, MD: National Association of School Psychologists.

SEVEN

TERMINATION

Every practicum must end and most often means a transition to a more advanced training experience for the school psychology candidate. It is a time for both supervisors and supervisees to celebrate the successes achieved during the practicum training and plan ahead for continued professional development. Supervisees must also say "goodbye" to the students, parents, and staff with whom they have developed relationships during the training, as well as end their relationship with their supervisor. While it is a natural and necessary transition for the trainee, the complexity of tasks and emotions may make it a somewhat overwhelming process in these final stages of the training. Supervisors can help to prepare trainees for a successful termination by helping them close casework, terminate professional relationships and building activities, and create a formal transition plan. This chapter discusses each of these supervision activities in detail.

CLOSING CASEWORK

Supervisees engage in a variety of case activities, including evaluations, consultation, direct academic or behavioral intervention and counseling, and work with a variety of clients (e.g., school staff, parents, students) during the practicum. Some of these activities are time limited (e.g., evaluations) while others require ongoing maintenance (e.g., consultation, counseling, academic, social, or behavioral intervention). As such, each type of casework requires unique termination activities. We focus our discussion in this chapter to the three most basic types of casework—evaluations, consultation, and counseling—and termination activities related to each.

Evaluations

Candidates complete a range of case study evaluations as part of practica experiences. Case study evaluations are relatively brief (e.g., 30–60 days), restricted to an individual client (student), and require a limited number of interactions with students, staff, and teachers. The purpose of the case study is to clearly identify student needs and abilities and to further inform the classroom practices necessary for the student to meaningfully participate in the curriculum. Thus, termination activities central to this type of work include: (a) appropriate documentation of the evaluation and results, (b) attention to student record keeping, and (c) overall management of program planning and intervention.

Case study evaluations are documented in school settings in both formal reports and in student individualized education programs (IEPs). As discussed in Chapter 3, practicum candidates should practice writing a full evaluation report and translating this information into the IEP paperwork. Teaching supervisees what to do with student records is also important. An educational record is defined by the Family Educational Rights and Privacy Act (FERPA) and the Individuals with Disabilities Education Improvement Act (IDEIA) as records, files, documents, and other materials that are directly related to a student and maintained by an educational agency or institution (FERPA, 2002; IDEIA, 2004). Some of the documents related to evaluation activities may be maintained in student files (e.g., reports, test summary forms), while others are maintained in personal files of the school psychologist (e.g., test protocols, interview forms, notes). While they may be stored in different locations within the school, each is an important part of the student record and must be made available to parents upon request. Supervisees must learn how to effectively store and organize the files to maintain careful documentation of student information and comply with federal regulations regarding such records. Supervisees should also pay close attention to termination activities related to student programming. Due to the nature of evaluation work, school psychologists can easily fall into a "test and place" habit, where work with the student ends in presentation of case study results in an IEP meeting and little, if any, follow-up is provided in terms of ensuring that interventions based on assessment results are implemented. School psychologists should help to ensure program and intervention success by providing any necessary training or support during the initial stages of treatment (e.g., preparation of intervention material, coaching), carefully monitoring student performance (progress monitoring), and assisting the school team in evaluating student outcomes and treatment effectiveness (e.g., formal review of the data every quarter).

Consultation

Practicum candidates may have an opportunity to provide consultation to teachers or parents regarding academic, behavioral, or social concerns for a variety of students during the training. As highlighted in Chapter 2, it is important to train candidates in one or more structured and empirically validated models of consultation during these early experiences. Most consultation models already attend specifically to termination as a key activity in the overall process. For example, in behavioral consultation, consultants arrange for termination with postimplementation planning during the problem evaluation interview (Bergan & Kratochwill, 1990). During termination, consultants may develop a maintenance plan for the consultees and inform them about how they may seek future support if issues resurface (e.g., leave their contact information, discuss the referral process). Consultants may also need to attend to the relationships they have developed and appropriately provide closure for consultees. A teacher who has worked collaboratively with a consultant for 3 months may suddenly miss the emotional and professional support offered through the consultation. Consultants should be careful, therefore, to adequately prepare consultees for upcoming termination activities (e.g., discuss termination process in advance, prepare consultee for termination timelines) and attend to any postconsultation resources that might be helpful (e.g., additional training, other personnel support available).

Counseling

While considerable attention has been provided in the literature to the issue of termination in therapy, much of this work is central to the fields of counseling and clinical psychology. Counseling in school settings is unique and actually quite different than that provided in other settings (e.g., mental health center, clinic, hospital). Often, school psychologists deliver counseling services in an individual or group therapy format to address goals and services that are part of a student's IEP. Counseling activities in school settings may require a wide range of techniques, theoretical orientations, assessment practices to identify student need and monitor progress; consultation with teachers and parents; crisis prevention and intervention; and social skills training (Plotts & Lasser, 2013). Lastly, the school context itself impacts how services are provided, with counseling sessions often being brief in terms of the length of individual sessions (e.g., 30 minutes or less) and number of sessions provided (e.g., 8-week group, individual student counseling for a quarter or semester).

Termination of counseling in school settings often occurs in response to natural transitions (e.g., end of group, close of the school year). Some practitioners are able to maintain relationships with the students they counsel by monitoring the generalization of their skills over time through consultation with teachers and parents, and have the ability to reinstate the counseling services they provide (e.g., after breaks, in response to new student needs). Practicum candidates who engage in counseling are at the site for a limited amount of time and often need to plan for forced termination, ending the relationship before the counselor or student is ready. Penn (1990) outlines several important steps to consider when handling forced termination in counseling. Those most relevant to counseling in school settings include the following: (a) informing the client before the start of termination, (b) leaving time for discussion, (c) facilitating expression of feelings, (d) recognizing indirect expressions or reactions, (e) summing it up, (f) transferring to a new counselor, and (g) facilitating a final ending. This information is expanded upon in the next section.

Supervision Activities for Closing Casework

While termination of casework may be most salient at the end of a school year when school staff prepare for a lengthy break, it is an activity that will occur each time the practicum candidate ends formal work with a particular student. Supervisors may, therefore, find it helpful to orient practicum candidates to termination procedures and resources in the earlier stages of the training experience. At a minimum, supervisors can help to prepare supervisees for more formal termination of casework about a month in advance of the end of the training. Supervisors may find the termination checklist for casework in Handout 7.1 useful in orienting supervisees to this process. The checklist is organized around the three main casework activities we outlined in this chapter—evaluations, consultation, and counseling. Supervisors and supervisees may find the checklist helpful in guiding their activities around termination and ensuring that appropriate steps have been taken to close student casework in the school setting.

In addition to a more general checklist for the termination of casework, we feel that special attention should be given to the end of counseling activities, given the level of direct work with students required in this role. Table 7.1 provides a list of field activities aligned to the selected termination recommendations from Penn (1990) discussed in the previous section. The table outlines seven considerations related to termination of counseling work, particularly as they relate to forced termination situations. Supervisors may direct trainees to create a formal termination plan for their counseling work at the start of individual and group counseling activities. The selected strategies can then be integrated into the student's formal treatment plan and monitored and maintained throughout the counseling work.

	HANDOUT 7.1 Termination Checklist for Casework
	Evaluations
☐	Place final report in student file, with all required signatures
☐	Document evaluation results and corresponding goals in student individualized education program (IEP), if relevant
☐	Store protocols, notes, and other assessment records in a secure location
☐	Develop any necessary tools and resources necessary for student interventions
☐	Provide training and consultation to school team regarding student interventions
☐	Identify data collection tools and methods required for progress monitoring performance
☐	Establish and communicate timelines for review of data
☐	Remove all personal notes and extraneous information from student records
☐	Share all passwords for electronic records and scoring programs with supervisor
	Consultation
☐	Develop necessary maintenance plans for consultees and clients
☐	Provide contact information and process to reinstate consultation, if necessary
☐	Document and share student outcome data with relevant school staff and parents
☐	Gather consultee outcome (e.g., satisfaction, treatment acceptability) data to inform future practice
☐	Provide consultee resources and materials relevant to work with student or future students
	Counseling
☐	Inform student(s), teachers, and parents of termination well in advance of final session
☐	Create formal termination plan, with timelines and activities identified
☐	Plan for transfer of counseling cases to other mental health providers (e.g., transfer records, document student progress and needs, facilitate meeting with student and new provider)
☐	Consult with parents and teachers regarding the end of counseling services
☐	Create a maintenance plan for new skills learned though counseling, including a helpful resource list that may be accessed in counselor's absence
☐	Finalize group and individual counseling case records, storing them in a secure location

TABLE 7.1 Steps to Termination in School-Based Counseling

Termination Recommendation	Activities
Inform students, teachers, and parents at the outset of treatment the anticipated date of termination	■ Include counseling duration in consent forms and process ■ Discuss counseling timeline in first session ■ Explore alternative treatments, if necessary, especially for students with more persistent mental health issues
Discuss the termination	■ Remind students, teachers, and parents of termination weeks or even a month in advance of end date ■ Discuss at beginning of session and allow time for discussion, questions, and the expression of feelings about the termination ■ Describe what termination will look like and feel like
Facilitate expression of feelings	■ Approach the topic with importance but do not act overly dramatic ■ Use "student-friendly" language to explore the issue (e.g., our last session will be …) ■ Ask how student(s) feel(s) about the end of counseling ■ Ask parents and teachers about their feelings regarding termination
Recognize indirect expressions or reactions	■ Be alert to behavioral (e.g., missing sessions, disruptive classroom behavior, lack of participation in session, dependency) or emotional changes (e.g., sad affect, anger) that may suggest termination is difficult for student ■ Further explore termination with student ■ Consult with teachers and parents regarding behavioral and/or emotional changes, creating support plans when necessary
Sum it up	■ Reflect on work that has been accomplished ■ Review goals and celebrate attainment of goals that have been met ■ Create a maintenance plan with student(s) and/or tools for use beyond formal therapy (e.g., coping tools kit)
Transfer to a new counselor	■ Transfer to a new counselor, if appropriate ■ Meet with new counselor to discuss work, progress, and current student needs ■ Facilitate one or two joint sessions with new counselor to help introduce student to new professional, establish trust, and facilitate rapport-building

(continued)

TABLE 7.1 Steps to Termination in School-Based Counseling (*continued*)	
Termination Recommendation	**Activities**
End with purpose	■ Leave student(s) with a "resource list" of support available in your absence ■ Facilitate a special activity or session to signify the end of the relationship and counseling (e.g., goal recognition party, fun game, or activity testing new skills)

Adapted from Penn (1990).

TERMINATING PROFESSIONAL RELATIONSHIPS AND BULDING ACTIVITIES

Trainees develop professional relationships with a variety of school personnel during the practicum training, such as teachers, related services personnel, administrators, and important staff (e.g., secretary, technology specialist). Many of these school personnel influence supervisee training both during the practicum and well beyond its end. For example, a school administrator may be involved in the potential hiring of a practicum candidate once he or she has formally entered the profession. Teachers and other school personnel may serve as key resources for other training opportunities as well (e.g., extend an invitation to introduce trainee to friends, family, and other professionals working in other educational settings). Supervisors should take time to discuss the importance of and strategies for maintaining these relationships over time. Ensuring that trainees terminate these relationships appropriately is one of the first steps in the maintenance of professional relationships beyond the training experience. Termination may include activities such as taking time to inform school staff about the trainee's final day, prompting the trainee to thank relevant school professionals for specific training opportunities, and ensuring that the trainee leaves resources, student files, and records with all relevant school personnel, to name a few. Supervisors should ultimately convey to trainees that professional relationships rarely end with each training experience and that they should be carefully maintained as part of overall professional development. One might imagine the types of opportunities lost (e.g., jobs, resources, special training) for a candidate that leaves important school professionals with either little to remember ("Who was she?") or negative things to say ("He was rude and didn't care about the school").

Supervisors should also attend to the termination of their own relationship with the supervisee. By the end of a practicum, some supervisors have spent up to an entire 9-month school year with a particular trainee. Both the supervisor and supervisee may find themselves relying on one another for professional (e.g., assistance, training) and personal (e.g., time with a like-minded companion, friendly conversation) support. Supervisors should discuss the end of the supervision relationship well in advance of the final days to help supervisees plan for the termination. Supervision topics may include logistics and planning for year-end activities; feedback regarding the supervision process and training; feedback regarding supervisee growth; sharing of resources; and the terms and parameters regarding the posttraining relationship. Each of these is explored further in the following section.

As a professional member of the school community, trainees should also consider all of the building processes and procedures that occur at the end of a school year or their training. For example, school personnel are often issued a school e-mail, building keys or badges, provided office space, and given other resources in order to complete their work each year. Practicum candidates may receive some of these resources as well and it is important to provide an orientation for all exit activities at the building level. At worst, you may find a trainee that has left important personal items in a locked desk drawer with no access until the end of the summer. Supervisees should consider all activities required to clean their office space and return appropriate building materials, as necessary.

Supervision Activities for Terminating Professional Relationships and Building Activities

Assisting trainees in terminating their professional relationships is an important supervision activity, as it is foundational to helping trainees understand the importance of professional networks and resources. Supervisors can first support this skill by modeling the importance of their own professional networks (e.g., using colleagues for support, eating lunch with other staff, taking time to greet school staff and teachers in the morning). Supervisors may want to consider how they can model these strategies in their own unique environments for trainees and also discuss these actions more openly during supervision. For example, a supervisors may ask a trainee to join him or her in "morning rounds" of the school, an activity where the supervisor walks through the building before first bell to greet staff, students, and other school personnel. The supervisor may later discuss this activity during individual supervision and its relevance to practice (e.g., informs others you are in the building today; helps you build personal relationships; encourages others to contact you for support).

Terminating the supervisory relationship should be a formal process that includes planning, discussion, and specific actions. Supervisors should take time to orient supervisees to the process of closing this relationship, allow for reflection of the experience, and aim to ensure that supervisor and supervisee have left the experience with a sense of its worth. Informing supervisees about the number of supervision sessions, activities, and level of support that will be available during the final month of the training can help to orient the trainee to the fact that this relationship is coming to an end. Also, it may be incredibly beneficial if the supervisor allocates one or more individual supervision sessions to reflection and feedback about the process. Supervisors may like feedback on how useful their supervision was for the trainees or whether the training opportunities provided were adequate, while supervisees may request feedback on their overall attainment of specific school psychological skills. Supervisors and supervisees should also consider what they have learned from one another through the shared experience. A practicing psychologist may want the trainee to share specific intervention resources or tools they have designed during the training. Trainees may request access to helpful report formats, templates, and other materials. Finally, supervisors should initiate a conversation about what type of relationship they may maintain with the trainee once the practicum has ended. Some supervisors may feel comfortable suggesting personal meetings (e.g., lunch date) after training has ended while others would prefer to maintain a strictly professional relationship. Trainees and supervisors should discuss and agree upon specific boundaries that will be maintained over time.

Supervisors will also need to assist trainees in identifying important termination activities related to overall building procedures. Supervisors who may be relatively new to a particular school building may not be fluent in building procedures themselves and will therefore best support trainees by connecting them with school staff that may be able to assist. For example, a supervisor may ask one of the school office personnel to mentor the trainee in these activities through the end of the training period and monitor these interactions through supervision with the candidate. Alternatively, some supervisors may be well versed in building procedures and processes and would rather monitor these activities more closely (e.g., hold a meeting with the on-site technology staff to plan for termination) or create a manual or guide for the student to use. Handout 7.2 is an organized checklist, reflecting the activities outlined in this section that supervisors might also consider using with trainees.

CREATING A TRANSITION PLAN

The termination of practicum training often signifies the transition to an advanced level of field work, most often the school psychology internship. Many supervisees have accepted internship offers and are beginning to plan for this new role. They will need to manage the anticipation of and

	HANDOUT 7.2 Termination Checklist for Professional Activities
	Relationships With Staff
☐	Inform school personnel of your final day
☐	E-mail school staff to provide contact information, including new e-mail address
☐	Provide training and/or leave resources with relevant staff to continue work
☐	Make personal requests for recommendation letters and references
☐	Thank relevant school personnel for collaboration, experience, and training
	Relationship With Supervisor
☐	Determine final day of training
☐	Request final feedback on growth and competence
☐	Provide feedback on training experience
☐	Discuss plan for posttraining contact (e.g., format, frequency)
☐	Request supervision or training materials and resources that will be helpful for future practice (e.g., forms, templates, intervention materials)
	Building Processes and Procedures
☐	Return and/or "clean up" computer, per guidelines from district technology support
☐	Terminate e-mail
☐	Determine procedures for returning school badge and/or keys
☐	Review all test kits and intervention materials to ensure they are complete
☐	Return district manuals, testing materials, and other resources to appropriate personnel
☐	Remove all personal items from desk and office space
☐	Change phone messages and web-based information relevant to you

preparation for the internship, as well as any final expectations for the practicum. Successful termination requires attention and planning, similar to a training contract or proposal that was developed at the beginning of the practicum experience. Supervisors may therefore find it useful to assist supervisees with termination activities by creating a formal transition plan that considers any final practicum activities, the processes and procedures required for internship, and the transition to a new training site (i.e., the internship).

Most often, a practicum ends with the natural close of the school year in late spring or early summer. Supervising school psychologists may find that their schedule is quite demanding as they try to wrap up casework and plan for the following school year. Many candidates will be prepared to assist supervisors with additional tasks and activities, thereby sharing some of the caseload. Supervisors may find, by the end of training, many practicum candidates are quite eager to take-on additional work and may actually quite helpful to them. Expectations for year-end casework and activities, however, should be clearly communicated and agreed upon, as they may be additional to what was already documented in the training plan. The terms for supervision should also be reviewed, as supervisees may be able to complete some activities with a fair amount of independence (e.g., familiar casework, observations) and others with more guidance and monitoring (e.g., new roles).

Trainees will also need to attend to processes and procedures required to finalize the practicum and prepare for the internship. Formal termination of the practicum may include submission of several documents to the training institution, such as a summative supervisor evaluation, log of hours in field site, and exit surveys. Candidates may also be required to submit paperwork that verifies eligibility for the internship, obtain a provisional license with various credentialing bodies (e.g., state board of education), or pass relevant licensing examinations (e.g., National Certification in School Psychology [NCSP] Praxis, state content exams) in order to advance to internship training. Field and university supervisors should mentor school psychology trainees in relevant professional requirements through proper orientation and monitoring of the completion of such activities.

Termination of the practicum should also include thoughtful preparation for site-specific expectations of the supervisee's new training placement. The majority of supervisees will need to orient themselves to a new school building, district, and supervisor with the start of the internship. Some candidates may even need to prepare to move to a new geographic location. Supervisors may consider how to prepare supervisees by focusing on both training and supervision needs. Specific supervision activities are explored further in the following section.

Supervision Activities for Creating a Transition Plan

Supervisors can begin transition planning with supervisees initially with a discussion about all year-end activities and casework. A review of the initial training plan or proposal may provide an excellent way to determine whether original training goals were met and how much additional time trainees will have to devote to additional responsibilities. Supervisors should help trainees identify a fair balance of work required in the site (e.g., assisting supervisor casework), work aligned to trainee interests (e.g., exploring new roles), and work valuable to the internship (e.g., role required in new site). For example, a site supervisor may request that the trainee assist with two case studies in the final few months of the training, while the supervisee requests experience with the school-wide behavior support team as a personal interest and the district autism program to prepare for this role on internship. It may be helpful to generate a list of all potential activities in these three categories and agree upon a few select items from each.

Earlier in this chapter, we discussed the importance of attending to the termination of the supervisory relationship. This activity can be extended further to include a discussion about the transition to a new supervisory relationship, as most practicum candidates will complete their internship under the supervision of a different practicing school psychologist. Supervisors may first prompt trainees to consider what aspects of their relationship were most beneficial to learning and development. Trainees may also be prompted to identify aspects of supervision that may be improved to enhance supervision further. Supervisors who have requested regular feedback regarding supervision throughout training with a tool such as the supervision feedback form in Handout 1.2 may review these data to initiate this discussion. Supervisors can then help the trainee identify how to advocate for specific activities and supports in the new supervisory relationship.

As noted in the previous section, a formal transition plan can be an incredibly useful supervision tool in the final stages of training. We recommend that supervisors collaborate with the supervisee to develop a plan that documents the activities discussed in this section. A sample transition plan is included in Handout 7.3.

EVALUATION OF SUPERVISEE

One of the final supervisory responsibilities is a summative evaluation of trainee competence and readiness for advancement. University supervisors should communicate with field supervisors several weeks in advance of final deadlines of submission of the evaluation, with particular consideration for appropriate use of the tool. Many evaluation tools are designed with

HANDOUT 7.3 Sample Transition Plan

Practicum Termination Activities

Task	Due Date
Complete behavior case study	4/11/16
Complete academic case study	4/30/16
Complete four final group counseling sessions	4/4/16, 4/11/16, 4/18/16, 4/25/16
Assist with benchmark assessment	Week of 4/15/16
Complete all items on termination checklist	5/1/16

Processes and Procedures for Internship

Task	Due Date
Pass state licensure exam	5/1/16
Pass praxis exam	6/1/16
Apply for provisional state license	7/1/16

Activities to Prepare for Internship Site

Task	Due
Participate in two PBIS meetings	4/1/16, 5/1/16
Observe autism evaluation	5/5/16
Visit new site/Shadow and observe	5/31/16

a combination of rating scales and qualitative questions. Field supervisors should have a clear understanding of how to accurately rate candidates, required versus optional components of the evaluation, and any qualitative information that should be included. The university supervisor may consider meeting with the field supervisor in a face-to-face meeting to discuss the tool, providing formal training or including detailed instructions with the tool before the evaluation period.

The end of the practicum training is an ideal time for formal communication between the university and site supervisors. University and field supervisors should consult about the candidate's progress during the training and his or her readiness for the internship. This may be completed via an on-site visit, an exit interview, or surveys. An on-site visit may include the supervisee as well and would likely center on his or her abilities as a school psychologist. Valuable information about the quality of the training site, university-based training, supervision, and the general practicum program can be obtained with a structured interview or surveys. University personnel may find this data useful for program planning and accreditation purposes. Practicing school psychologists may use it as an opportunity to share important information about current issues in the field and request resources from the university.

SUPERVISOR TO-DO LIST

☐ Orient supervisee to termination checklist for casework
☐ Orient supervisee to termination checklist for professional activities
☐ Prepare trainee for transition to internship
☐ Create a transition plan for internship in a formal document

REFERENCES

Bergan, J. R., & Kratochwill, T. R. (1990). *Behavioral consultation in applied settings.* New York, NY: Plenum Press.

Family Educational Rights and Privacy Act. (2002). Title 34, Code of Federal Regulations—34 CFR Part 99.

Individuals with Disabilities Education Improvement Act. (2007). Title 34, Code of Federal Regulations—34 CFR Part 300.

Penn, L. S. (1990). When the therapist must leave: Forced termination of psychodynamic therapy. *Professional Psychology: Research and Practice, 21*(5), 379–384.

Plotts, C., & Lasser, J. (2013). *School psychology as counselor: A practitioner's handbook.* Bethesda, MD: National Association of School Psychologists.

EIGHT

ENHANCING TRAINING THROUGH COLLABORATION

Merriam-Webster's (2016) definition for *collaborate* is "to work with another person or group in order to achieve or do something." Implicit within this definition is an understanding that in order to accomplish certain pursuits, we must rely upon others to help us do so. Moreover, effective collaboration is voluntary, requires equality among participants, is based on mutual goals, requires the sharing of resources, and depends on shared responsibility for participation, decision making, and outcomes (Friend & Cook, 2007). These characteristics are woven through our discussion in this chapter, as we explore how practicum training may be enhanced through effective collaboration between trainers and field supervisors.

COLLABORATION

Successful practicum training requires strong collaboration between the trainee's university or institution and the supervising field psychologist. University personnel are ultimately responsible for the training of each candidate and direct many practicum activities. This direction is often offered through a list of requirements (e.g., number of hours, specific experiences, and activities) or via various course assignments (e.g., consultation project, intervention case study). Given the primary role of the university in practicum training, field supervisors typically find their main responsibility is to facilitate the expectations and requirements of the home institution. Once these obligations are met, many field supervisors try to further enhance training for individual candidates by creating experiences that are unique to their setting and/or of particular interest to the trainee. What results is a complex interaction between the university, field site, and supervisee. These interactions are enhanced through collaboration and communication that is oriented to candidate training. Successful collaboration between the university and field site includes consideration of site development and maintenance, effective communication, and training and support across settings. These topics are explored further in the following sections.

Site Development and Maintenance

Field placement and coordination play a critical role in the training of school psychologists. As such, many school psychology programs have an identified faculty position for this purpose. The individual fulfilling this role may be recognized with a variety of formal titles, such as field placement coordinator, clinical professor, or director of clinical training (DCT). For the purposes of this discussion, we will use the term DCT to refer to this position. One of the primary responsibilities of the DCT is the coordination and supervision of practica-related activities, including the placement of candidates in appropriate training sites. At the specialist level of training in school psychology, this requires facilitating placement largely in school-based sites, whereas this may be extended to other positions at the doctoral level, including clinics, hospitals, university, and private practice settings. While we focus our discussion on school-based sites, the material we present in this section can be easily applied to alternative practica settings as well.

Building networks and relationships

Many university programs have well-established practicum sites where they place new trainees with experienced supervisors as each new practicum begins. This may be particularly true for programs that are located in regions of the country where both trainees and high-quality sites are located in close proximity to the training institution. Some DCTs may find they need to develop sites more frequently due to the changing needs of trainees (e.g., geography) and of sites (e.g., personnel changes, lack of resources). In addition, some school districts have well-organized training programs, with key personnel responsible for facilitating practicum and internship programs. Many school psychologists, however, independently supervise candidates with little structure or support from the district. Unlike the internship, which is highly regulated in the field of school psychology, practices related to practicum vary significantly by training institution and region. The challenge for many university and school personnel responsible for developing practicum, therefore, is determining fit between site, training program, and individual trainees.

Site development begins by first developing a relationship between university and school personnel. Spending time fostering relationships with the right individuals is therefore important. While there are a number of ways to start exploring potential connections (e.g., cold calls, convenience, location), the most successful relationships may be developed through professional networks (e.g., colleagues, professional organizations, alumni training institutions). Remember, one of the central goals is establishing a training partnership that is a good fit for the university, site, and trainee. Box 8.1 includes a list of ways to build a professional network for site development, and separate activities are delineated for both university and school personnel. Once you have established who you want to connect with, it is important to also consider how best to make an introduction. While it is true various relationships may begin in any number of ways (e.g., personal meeting, phone call, e-mail contact), both university and school personnel should be cautious to respect any existing protocols that should be followed. For example, some school districts require that key administrators (e.g., director of psychological services, building principal) make decisions about training partnerships when they are responsible for supervising the district school psychologists. In some situations, these same administrators may actually be involved quite actively in recruitment activities, such as interviewing and selecting candidates, and making placements with supervising school psychologists. We suggest using the protocols in Box 8.2 when exploring site partnerships. Separate protocols are provided for both site and university personnel.

Establishing agreements and partnerships

Once the relationship has been developed with a particular training site or institution, key personnel should discuss the benefits and expectations for a potential partnership. For example, university personnel may discuss

---

BOX 8.1   Building Networks for Site Development

University Personnel	School District Personnel
Contact former colleagues in field	Contact alumni training institution
Connect local and regional districts	Contact other regional training programs
Connect with state school psychology organization	Connect with state school psychology organization
Connect with training faculty from related programs of study	Attend university job and placement fairs
Contact former trainees	

BOX 8.2 Protocol for Initiating Contact With New Site/University

University Protocol for Contacting Sites	Site Protocol for Contacting Training Programs
Step 1: Gain support from administration for site development; initial contact may be made with the building principal or district coordinator of psychological services	*Step 1*: Gain support from program or training director (e.g., department chair, director of clinical training)
Step 2: Identify qualified school psychologist(s) in district to supervise	*Step 2*: Request information about practicum program, including structure, requirements, and candidate qualifications
Step 3: Discuss expectations for partnership	*Step 3*: Discuss expectations for partnership
Step 4: Establish training agreement	*Step 4*: Establish training agreement

potential resources (e.g., access to test kits, professional development, continuing education credits) that would be available to the site in return for on-site trainee supervision with qualified school psychologists. Site personnel may wish to outline the unique experiences and activities that would be available to trainees and make requests for particular types of candidates (e.g., specific level of experience, professional characteristics) or supervision from the university. It is important to outline expectations for all involved, including university, site, and trainee.

University and site personnel should consider establishing a formal training agreement that can codify the partnership. This may be separate from or combined with the training plan that was discussed in Chapter 1. Training agreements serve as a contract between the university, site, and trainee and outline the requirements, responsibilities, and contributions of each. Some agreements may also include a specific plan for the trainee. Common components of an individual training plan include: (a) a description of how a trainee's time is allocated; (b) goals and objectives of the practicum; (c) methods of evaluation of a trainee's performance; (d) nature of supervision; (e) form and frequency of feedback from the agency/supervisor to training faculty; and (f) rationale for experience and assurance that the practicum is organized, sequential, and meets the needs of the trainee (Association of State and Provincial Psychology Boards [ASPPB], 2009). Both the university and site may have separate contracts that outline the training partnership. Given that the agreement serves as a contract, it is recommend that university and school personnel appropriately seek counsel with legal representatives available to them in the university or district to ensure that it complies with organizations procedures and policies, as well as any relevant regulatory standards. A sample agreement is provided in Appendix E.

Communication

Effective communication between university and site supervisors is critical to the success of a practicum partnership and the training of individual candidates. *Effective* communication occurs when the individual receiving the message clearly understands the message conveyed by the individual sending the information. What this suggests is that supervisors need to attend to both *what* messages are sent and received, as well as *how* these messages are conveyed. We address both of these issues further, as it relates to practicum training.

Supervisors should first consider *what* needs to be communicated during the practicum training. For example, university personnel need to inform site supervisors about training expectations and requirements for the practicum candidate (e.g., number of hours, required activities) and site supervisor (e.g., qualifications, supervision activities), while site supervisors need to effectively communicate about supervisee progress over the course of training. Of course, supervisors may also find that they need to communicate about other training-related issues as they arise, such as opportunities for supervisor or trainee professional development, unique training situations (e.g., supervisor's or trainee's medical leave or accommodations), or the need for trainee remediation. Identifying what needs to be communicated between site and university during the early stages of training will help set the stage for a meaningful partnership. For example, university supervisors may send a simple e-mail in the early fall to introduce themselves to site supervisors and provide contact information and availability for ongoing communication. They may also take time to carefully convey their supervisory responsibilities (e.g., weekly seminar, review of casework, schedule for site visits) for the training to clearly acknowledge that supervision is a shared partnership. Site supervisors may find it helpful to share information about the unique characteristics of the training site and ensure that it is an appropriate fit for the trainee. To summarize, field training communications are typically oriented around three main areas: (a) university expectations and requirements, (b) supervisor qualifications and requirements, and (c) trainee progress (e.g., strengths and limitations).

Communication between university and site supervisors is a two-way process, requiring each to attend to *how* they send and receive messages. With technology becoming increasingly more sophisticated, information can be shared in many formats, including face-to-face, telephone, e-mail, text messaging, videoconferencing, electronic portfolios, training database, instant messaging, memos, letters, webpages, and documents. Some or all of these methods may be acceptable for particular sites and universities and depend on the content of messages, technology skills of supervisors, resources (e.g., access to technology, print materials, database accounts), and supervisor preferences. University personnel should plan to provide training and support to enable site supervisors to use specific communications effectively. For example, an institution that uses an online database to manage training documents (e.g., supervisor evaluations) may distribute a database manual, provide on-site or web-based (e.g., webinar) training, and call all site supervisors early in the year to ensure they know how to use the training database. While the practicum candidate may also be responsible for relaying many messages (e.g., communicating required activities), supervisors should also plan for direct communication between the site and university to ensure there is clarification and support, when necessary.

In addition to knowing the content and methods for sharing information, supervisors should also attend to the timelines of important communications. Some practicing school psychologists may not receive a more personal communication (e.g., phone call, e-mail, in-person meeting) from university personnel until it is time to evaluate the trainee at the midterm (e.g, December) or, even worse, year-end. Conversely, there may be times when university personnel struggle to get site supervisors to respond to inquiries or share rich information about a particular candidate or training at the site. In our experience, both university and field personnel feel reluctant to reach out to one another regarding training at times, because they do not want to overly burden the other with minor issues, questions, or concerns. This is particularly problematic when there are concerns about the trainee's performance, even if they are minor in nature, as it delays problem solving, support, and remediation, if necessary. Identifying a schedule for communication at the forefront of training is therefore highly recommended. University personnel can take the lead in this planning by identifying a more general communication plan that will be used with all site personnel and make minor modifications with individual sites as needed (e.g., preferred contact methods for individual supervisors, frequency based on candidate needs). A sample list of communications is included in Table 8.1 for illustration.

Training and Support Across Settings

Successful practicum training requires careful maintenance of the partnerships developed between the university and field site. At a minimum, this includes adherence to and monitoring of any training contracts established

TABLE 8.1   Sample Communications Between University and Site

Communication	Method	Timeline
Site/supervisor requirements	Meeting or e-mail	August
Training manual	Word document or PDF sent via e-mail; post on training webpage	August
Practicum syllabus	e-mail	Each term
Training agreement or plan	Meeting or e-mail	September
Introductory e-mail	e-mail	August
Training for database (e.g., evaluation tools, forms)	Manual	August
Site visit(s)	On-site meeting	Fall, winter, spring
Invitation for supervisor training	Electronic flyer or invitation; e-mail	Winter
Field training newsletter	Webpage and e-mail	Monthly
Correspondence regarding supervisor evaluation of candidate performance	e-mail	November and March
Documentation of supervision (continuing education)	Letter sent via e-mail	May

between the university and site. Site and university personnel, however, should consider extending the focus beyond simple maintenance by identifying ways to offer support across settings to enhance candidate training. Universities are resource-rich institutions that may offer practitioners access to a range of resources (e.g., assessment materials, interventions, library materials) and professional development opportunities (e.g., training, books, articles). Many supervisors would likely agree that one of the perks of supervising candidates-in-training is access to the *best practices* and *cutting-edge technologies* in the field. Likewise, training faculty often has much to learn from practitioners in the field, such as important feedback on regional practice, resources, and trends. University and field personnel should consider how to maximize the resources across settings, thereby improving candidate training and the overall impact to the schools and students served. We feel there are a variety of ways to build support across settings and particular activities are often specific to the unique needs of a given partnership. As such, we provide a list of potential activities in Box 8.3 for consideration.

BOX 8.3   Building Support Across Training Settings

University	Field Site
Provide free professional development aligned to faculty expertise to offer continuing education for supervisors	Facilitate opportunities for applied research
Provide a series of supervision meetings for field supervisors	Invite training faculty to professional development offered through district
Offer field supervisors access to university library, including online account to search databases	Invite training faculty to important district meetings (e.g., school board, staff meetings, district task force, advisory boards)
Provide access to test kits and/or assessment materials available to department	Share manuals and publications that outline district policies, procedures, and initiatives
Provide supervisors monetary compensation	
Provide continuing education credits per state or National Association of School Psychologists (NASP) guidelines	

To enhance the training and consistency across sites, university personnel may also consider establishing a forum to provide metasupervision, a format that is recognized in the training of supervisors (Liddle, Breunlin, Schwartz, & Constantine, 1984) and becoming increasingly more popular as a training component in supervision courses at the graduate level (Lyon, Heppler, Leavitt, & Fisher, 2008). Metasupervision has been described as a process whereby a senior professional provides guidance on supervision to a more junior psychologist who is supervising trainees (Keenan-Miller & Corbett, 2015). Field and university psychologists alike will have a range of experience in the supervision of school psychology candidates, as well as formal training in supervision, and expertise in certain topics may shift to different individuals, at times (e.g., supervising bilingual psychologist may have expertise in supervising bilingual candidates, university supervisor may have expertise in general supervision and training). As such, we suggest a more flexible approach to metasupervision with colleagues and provide information about two potential formats.

In the first format, university personnel may facilitate metasupervision for all field practitioners by offering a regular meeting or seminar to support supervision in the field. For example, field supervisors may meet monthly with the university trainer to discuss supervision through presentations, readings, and informal discussions. The university trainer may lead these activities and align the content to the specific training concerns of program candidates (e.g., facilitation of course assignments, development of specific skills in training curriculum). In this format, the university trainer largely offers guidance and metasupervision to field supervisors. The second format considers the range of skills and expertise in the larger group of supervisors. The university trainer may establish a metasupervision format where individual supervisors may be identified as the metasupervisor for the group for a specific topic. For example, a practicing bilingual psychologist may provide metasupervision on issues related to training in cultural competence. The benefit of this format is, of course, the ability to maximize the resources of the group, but is also somewhat dependent on the specific skills of those involved.

COMMON ISSUES

The majority of practicum candidates will progress in their training without significant issues, making it an overall positive experience for all involved in the practicum. At times, however, supervisors and supervisees run into difficulties or challenges that require reflection, assessment, and attention. Challenges may include issues related to the trainee specifically (e.g., lack of skill, lack of professional behavior), to the supervisory relationship (e.g., poor match), or to the field training demands and requirements (e.g., course assignments, licensing requirements). Moreover, when difficulties do arise, they are often very taxing on the time, energy, and motivation of field supervisors and university trainers. Having a proactive approach to problematic behaviors that considers both the prevention of and response to difficulties is important to supervision. In this chapter, we focus our discussion on how supervisors can address trainee problems of professional competence, develop and use remediation plans successfully, and help trainees balance fieldwork with coursework.

Professional Competence Problems

An understanding of what is meant by professional competence is important for this discussion. Willis and Dubin (1990) suggest two broad domains of professional competence—*proficiencies* and *general characteristics*. Proficiencies relate to discipline-specific knowledge and skills, while general characteristics refer to individual abilities, traits, motivation, attitude, and values. As they relate to the field of school psychology, we think of these two domains as relating to professional skills (e.g., report writing, knowledge of assessment and intervention) and professional behaviors (e.g., personal dispositions, interpersonal skills, ethical and legal behaviors). Although research in this area is quite limited, training institutions have reported that the most common professional competency problems are clinical deficiencies (e.g., issues with skill acquisition), interpersonal problems, issues in supervision, and personality disorders (Forrest, Elman, Gizara, & Vacha-Hasse, 1999).

Resolving professional competence problems that may arise during the practicum can be quite challenging to a supervisor. Trainees begin the practicum with a range of preparation via coursework and variable exposure to professional settings and, more specifically, school settings. Moreover, the connection or relationship the supervisor has to the training program may vary somewhat across sites and training institutions. Supervisors who feel disconnected to training programs may feel that they are underprepared to really understand what competence looks like in a supervisee and may be reluctant to address a problem when it arises. Supervisors who view themselves, and are themselves viewed by the training program, as an integral component of the training experience may feel more competent and empowered to solve skill and performance issues. We provide a summary of some common issues that arise during the practicum training as it relates to professional skills and behaviors and the supervision strategies to address each in Table 8.2. These will be discussed in the following sections more thoroughly.

Resolving skill issues

As presented in Table 8.2, some common professional skill problems that supervisees may present during the practicum experience may include inadequate content knowledge, application issues, and dependence on the supervisor. While in some ways providing support to address trainee issues with content knowledge may be quite straightforward (i.e., teach skill), it may feel particularly frustrating for field supervisors and university trainers alike, as it is often expected that trainees have adequate content knowledge in specific domains (e.g., intellectual and achievement assessment) before beginning the practicum. Field supervisors who have knowledge of the trainee's overall coursework sequence, including current courses and expectations, will be better equipped to gauge what candidates should know before the practicum begins. Some suggested supervision activities to address trainee issues with content include providing additional professional development (e.g., training), assigning articles and resources for review, requiring trainees to audit content courses (e.g., intellectual assessment course), and providing additional practice opportunities (e.g., supervised testing). For example, a candidate who continues to make errors when scoring test protocols may

TABLE 8.2   Common Trainee Issues and Supervision Strategies

	Specific Problem	Supervision Strategies
Professional skills	Inadequate content knowledge	Assign readings
		Facilitate professional development and training
		Require trainee to audit content course
	Application issues	Normalize experience
		Prompt integration of conceptual and practical skills
		Provide additional supervised opportunities
	Dependence	Provide frequent pre- and postsupervision feedback
Professional behaviors	Organization	Clarify expectations
		Demand accountability
		Share tools and approach
	Interpersonal skills	Prompt reflective practice
		Help connect ineffective behaviors to impact on work
		Share effective strategies and approach
	Accepting feedback	Normalize experience
		Support response
		Prompt reflective practice

be required to audit select class sessions of a university assessment course while also completing several key assessments with students under the direct observation of the field supervisor.

Practica represent the first formal field training for school psychology trainees in many institutions. It is the first time trainees have the opportunity to apply the theoretical concepts learned through coursework under the supervision of a licensed and practicing school psychologist. Supervisees may have difficulty applying different methods or models in their field settings and require assistance understanding how conceptual academic models are applied. Supervisors may first address trainee issues with application by helping the trainee understand that it is quite typical to experience such challenges, thereby normalizing the experience. Additionally, supervisors should take time to prompt the integration of conceptual and practical concepts more regularly. For example, a supervisor may review the steps of problem identification with a trainee before participating in a data review meeting with the problem solving team and take time after the meeting to discuss how all steps were applied in that particular experience. While doing so, it is important to explicitly highlight examples of specific methods (e.g., "We used the CBM-R benchmark data to determine whether the student is discrepant from his peers"). Trainees will also benefit from additional supervised opportunities to practice integrating their theoretical knowledge into practice and generalize their skills to various situations. For example, candidates often administer multiple batteries of the same types of tests to students who are usually considered average or above average performers as part of the requirement for many assessment courses. Interpretation of the results may be somewhat limited and supervisees are often provided with a report template or model from the instructor or textbook. When asked to assess a student suspected of having a learning disability and use a new report format in the field, trainees may easily become overwhelmed with the complexity of interpretation and documentation required for the case.

As novice supervisees, practicum trainees spend a great deal of time under the direct supervision of the field supervisor. Some trainees may find it difficult to increase independence when it is expected and become overly dependent on the supervisor for direction with completing tasks. Issues with dependence can be an extension of the trainee's difficulty applying concepts in the field (e.g., difficulty with case conceptualization in the site) or related to concerns about overstepping boundaries with the supervisor (e.g., view this as their supervisor's role). For example, a supervisee may be tentative to complete a well-known task without getting approval from the supervisor first for fear of making a mistake. Frequent pre- and post session supervision can be an excellent supervisory tool to help trainees develop more independence. For example, if a supervisee is waiting to be assigned components of an initial evaluation, a supervisor can prompt the supervisee to complete an assessment plan that identifies the referral question(s), assessment methods, and timeline for completion. After the supervisee completes the evaluation and initial report, the supervisor can provide follow-up supervision to address areas of strength and those requiring improvement.

Resolving comportment issues

Resolving trainee problems with professional behaviors are often more difficult, as they are considered more personal in nature and, at times, not easily taught or practiced. Imagine a trainee who has a somewhat awkward social demeanor and has been observed to struggle in communications with school staff. The field supervisor may feel quite reluctant to discuss this concern with the trainee, as it may feel like a criticism of the trainee's overall personality and likability. The supervisor may also struggle to identify strategies to support the trainee and help the trainee improve relationships with school staff. Supervisors should remember, as psychologists, their expertise in addressing challenging behaviors applies to adults as well as children. Prevention and early intervention are emphasized, as well as a positive approach to supporting preferred behaviors and focusing on a supervisee's strengths as well as difficulties. Common comportment issues that supervisees may present during the practicum include organization and time management issues, interpersonal difficulties, and difficulties accepting feedback. Resolving these issues may be beyond the skill or influence of the supervisor if these are long-standing habits. With less severe problems, a gentle prompt or reminder about expected behaviors may be all that is needed. With more persistent and pervasive issues, a formal remediation plan between the field site and training institution may be necessary.

The initial practicum experience can be difficult to navigate and organize as trainees try to balance their graduate coursework, time spent in the field setting, and any outside demands such as family, work, and personal responsibilities. This can present a real challenge for supervisees who are new to the professional world and quite used to following a more structured schedule (e.g., weekly class meetings, syllabi, assignments). It is also important to recognize that trainees are part of a cohort of candidates while in training and some candidates rely on the "groupthink" approach to manage expectations and deadlines. Understanding the group and generational norms for certain behaviors may be useful. Is there a popular type of planner (e.g., electronic, paper) to organize their schedule or coursework? As a first step, a supervisor should provide clear expectations for deadlines and products, as well as demand accountability. In many cases, supervisors only have to do this one time to be effective. Supervisors should also share their tools and resources for staying organized and meeting deadlines, as well as emphasizing that this a critical skill for being an effective school psychologist. For example, supervisors may demonstrate how they use Outlook or Google calendar to maintain their daily schedule.

Resolving a trainee's interpersonal difficulties can be challenging for a supervisor, due to the discomfort a supervisor may feel providing feedback on the trainee's personal characteristics (e.g., personality), as well as the strain it may place on the overall relationship between supervisor and supervisee (e.g., fear that the trainee will feel that he or she is not well liked). Supervisors may approach interpersonal difficulties by providing opportunities for reflective practice and helping trainees understand how the interpersonal issue may impact their work as a school psychologist. A trainee who acts timid when interacting with teachers and school staff, for example, may benefit from specific feedback (e.g., "I have noticed that you struggle to communicate with some of the school staff") and examples of the difficulty (e.g., "Yesterday, you stood outside of Ms. Brooks door for 10 minutes before trying to gain her attention"), as well as opportunities for reflective practice (e.g., "Why do you think this may be happening?"). Helping a supervisee learn to use empathy when working with a teacher or parent may also help to address interpersonal difficulties. For example, a trainee who is viewed by teachers as a "know it all" may be asked to reflect upon experiences where he or she minimized teacher or parent concerns (e.g., "You should just give him more positive feedback") and consider (a) how likely it is that the supervisee would accept his or her own advice and, most importantly (b) identify how that advice or solution would make the supervisee feel.

Another common difficulty in supervision is a supervisee's difficulty with accepting feedback. It is important to recognize that many supervisees, at this point in training, have received only summative feedback as part of their coursework. These summative evaluations come in the form of mid-term and final grades, individual assignment grades, and the evaluation of other work products. For some trainees, a supervisor's evaluation of competencies may be the first formative, performance evaluation they have received.

All feedback provided to a supervisee should be documented and used as a tool to change performance. Supervision sessions should include a review of prior feedback and how it has been used to maintain or improve performance. Some supervisees may struggle to accept or meaningfully use corrective feedback that is provided in the field site, particularly if it is incongruent with their own perceptions of performance. Supervisors can employ a number of strategies to improve trainees' ability to accept feedback. First, supervisors should prepare trainees for feedback by informing them about feedback methods (i.e., how it will be provided) and timelines (i.e., when it will be provided) at the beginning of the practicum. Supervisees who are prepared for feedback (e.g., "I know I will get feedback when I submit each report for review") and can readily identify when they are receiving it (e.g., "This was feedback about my performance and not a suggestion about the meeting, in general") will have less uncertainty and anxiety about their performance. There is a range of feedback that may be provided during the practicum, including praise for individual activities (e.g., reports, meeting summaries), constructive feedback meant to improve performance (e.g., report revisions, suggestions for meeting presentations), and summative evaluations shared with the training institution. Supervisors can carefully review all forms of feedback available to trainees during the practicum and help them understand how valuable all of this information is to their development and future performance as psychologists.

When trainees struggle to accept feedback, supervisors should directly discuss these challenges with the supervisees and allow them to reflect on why the feedback is not being accepted. Supervisors may find it useful to ask the supervisee to assess the supervisor's feedback in the form of a rating scale. An example rating form is included in Handout 8.1. The supervisee and supervisor complete the rating scale together and, based on student responses, different strategies can be identified. For example, if a supervisee rates feedback as highly difficult to hear, the feedback may not be consistent with his or her self-evaluation or it may be new information. A supervisor can then help a supervisee explore the discrepancy between the self-evaluation and the supervisor's evaluation and develop strategies to bring them into congruence.

Remediation Plans

If trainee difficulties persist, and it becomes clear that informal support is not effective in improving supervisee performance, a formal remediation plan may need to be developed to address the specific skill or comportment issue. A formal remediation plan should be developed in partnership with the university training site and, in most cases, will be consistent with university program policy. Remediation plans should be in writing, identify the specific behaviors or skills that need to be changed, identify strategies that will be used to address the difficulties, and include a time frame for improvement (Cruise & Swerdlik, 2010). Field supervisors may be asked to provide data or strategies that have been used to address the difficulties in the site. Regular, specific supervision notes will help to support development of skills and remediation of trainee difficulties. Trainers and field supervisors should consider what supports in each setting might be necessary for supervisee success. For example, a trainee who is having difficulty using professional communications in the field site may send all e-mail communications to the university advisor for review and feedback before sending to site personnel, while the field supervisor may assist in providing support with on-site personal communications. The roles and responsibilities of all individuals involved should be specified clearly within the plan.

When remediation is necessary, it is important to draft a plan for the trainee that focuses on trainee skill development and growth (Cruise & Swerdlik, 2010). The ultimate training goal is not to document and monitor concerns, but rather to provide the trainee with opportunity and support for professional development. We suggest that trainers and field supervisors consider this more positive approach even when describing the process of remediation with candidates. The term *remediation* tends to invoke a negative connotation, regardless of the actual meaning ("to remedy").

HANDOUT 8.1   Feedback Rating and Response Scale

1. This feedback was difficult to receive   1   2   3   4   5

If above a 3, explain why (i.e., not consistent with my evaluation of my skills, this is new, critical):

2. This feedback was specific   1   2   3   4   5

If below a 3, what other information is needed for understanding?

3. This feedback provides options for new skills   1   2   3   4   5

If below a 3, what other information is needed for understanding?

Supervisors should consider using terms that may carry a more positive tone (e.g., development plan, training support plan) when discussing such plans with trainees. This mere shift in language may make the trainee more receptive to support and invested in the process. Trainees should also have the opportunity to provide input during development of the plan. Some candidates may have meaningful insight to share about their difficulties and offer excellent suggestions about the resources that will help them make improvements, while other candidates may struggle to actively contribute to plan development.

Balancing Fieldwork With Coursework

While supervisors are valuable contributors to the training experience, they are also members of a professional school staff. Most practicum supervisors receive little if any compensation (e.g., monetary, time allocated for supervision) for their time in supervision. Balancing job responsibilities, as well as a novice trainee's site (e.g., casework) and university activities (e.g., coursework assignments), may be challenging at times, especially in the initial stages of the practicum. These issues may be best addressed by fostering trainee accountability and through active collaboration between university trainers and field supervisors.

University trainers should carefully instruct trainees in how to communicate with field supervisors and other school personnel about course projects and assignments. This may include guidelines for finding casework (e.g., who candidates should seek out in the field site, types of cases that may be most appropriate), issues related to consent procedures, and potential challenges they may encounter (e.g., school/district may not readily offer this opportunity). Trainers should offer this support when work is first assigned and be careful to monitor candidate performance over time (e.g., weekly project/case consultation). In addition, trainers may consider using more flexible assignment requirements, at times. For example, trainees may be encouraged to seek out opportunities in their practicum site for a particular assignment, but also have the option to complete a simulated activity or work on an applied project in another setting (e.g., university clinic, alternate site).

Field supervisors should prompt supervisees early in the training to share information about all course syllabi, assignments, and other relevant training requirements so that they can adequately prepare for the trainees' field experiences. Supervisees may fail to share this information readily for a variety of reasons (e.g., fear of overwhelming the field supervisors, view that some university requirements are distinct from field site and unimportant to supervisor, lack of planning and awareness). When this information is presented early, field supervisors have more time to plan, are more aware of opportunities that may be beneficial, and can problem solve any potential challenges. Supervisees may also be reluctant to approach individual teachers or staff for student data, case study information, or to participate in individual projects. Supervisors should consider ways to make initial trainee efforts successful, such as suggesting they connect with teachers that are effective collaborators or more open to working with a trainee. Supervisors are less likely to spend additional time addressing issues that delay assignment completion (e.g., teacher/staff resistance) if the supervisee gets off to a good start with teachers or other school staff. Finally, it is important to review trainee requirements and expectations regularly during formal supervision sessions to monitor completion and address problems proactively as they arise.

SUPERVISOR TO-DO LIST

- ☐ Build professional training networks
- ☐ Establish site agreements
- ☐ Establish methods, timelines, and content for communications between site and university
- ☐ Identify supervision and training support across settings
- ☐ Identify strategies to prevent trainee problems of professional competence
- ☐ Identify strategies to address trainee problems of professional competence
- ☐ Prepare a format for formal remediation, if it is necessary
- ☐ Identify strategies to support a healthy balance between trainee coursework and casework

REFERENCES

Association of State and Provincial Psychology Boards. (2009). *Guidelines on practicum experience for licensure*. Peachtree, GA: Author.

Collaborate. (2015). In *Merriam-Webster*. Retrieved from http://www.merriam-webster.com/dictionary/collaboration

Cruise, T. K., & Swerdlik, M. E. (2010). Problematic behaviors: Mediating differences and negotiating change. In J. Kaufman, T. L. Hughes, & C. A. Riccio (Eds.), *Handbook of education, training, and supervision of school psychologists in school and community* (Vol. 2, pp. 129–152). New York, NY: Routledge.

Forrest, L., Elman, N., Gizara, S., & Vach-Haase, T. (1999). Trainee impairment: Identifying, remediating, and terminating impaired trainees in psychology. *Clinical Psychologist, 27*, 627–686.

Friend, M., & Cook, L. (2007). *Interactions: Collaboration skills for school professionals* (5th ed.). Boston, MA: Pearson/Allyn & Bacon.

Keenan-Miller, D., & Corbett, H. I. (2015). Metasupervision: Can students be safe and effective supervisors? *Training and Education in Professional Psychology, 9*(4), 315–321. doi:10.1037/tep0000090

Liddle, H. A., Breunlin, D. C., Schwartz, R. C., & Constantine, J. A. (1984). Training family therapy supervisors: Issues of content, form and context. *Journal of Marital and Family Therapy, 10*(2), 139–150.

Lyon, R. C., Heppler, A., Leavitt, L., & Fisher, L. (2008). Supervisory training experiences and overall supervisory development in predoctoral interns. *Clinical Supervisor, 27*, 268–284. http://dx.doi.org/10.1080/07325220802490877

Willis, S. L., & Dubin, S. S. (Eds.). (1990). *Maintaining professional competence.* San Francisco, CA: Jossey-Bass.

PRACTICUM CANDIDATE EVALUATION FORM

Trainee Name: _____   Practicum Site: _____

Site Supervisor: _____   University Supervisor: _____

Semester of Evaluation: _____   Date of Evaluation: _____

Total Numbers of Hours Completed: _____

In accordance with previous Illinois State Board of Education (ISBE) School Psychology Standards and current 2010 National Association of School Psychologists (NASP) Standards, the following identifies those competency developments that are expected of the practicum school psychologist at the conclusion of the practicum year. The intent of the list of indicators is to provide guidelines regarding specific skill areas and an evaluative barometer to measure professional *growth at the stage of training at which the evaluation takes place*. Please rate only those areas relevant to the student's work.

Does not demonstrate competence: Student does not demonstrate the basic behaviors or steps associated with the skill or the student demonstrates the skill at a level that is ineffective for the client/condition.

Demonstrates minimal competence: Student demonstrates the skill at a very basic level, but a significant level of supervision is necessary in order for the skill to be effective.

Demonstrates emerging competence: Student demonstrates all aspects of the skill. The skill would be effective at a minimal level without supervision. Supervision is required to affirm the student's skill or to provide suggestions to increase the effectiveness of the skill.

Demonstrates preinternship competence: Student demonstrates all aspects of the skill and supervision is not needed to ensure skill effectiveness.

(continued)

PRACTICUM CANDIDATE EVALUATION FORM (*continued*)

Performance Indicators (Please place a check mark in the box that indicates current student performance on each indicator identified in the following.)	Does Not Demonstrate Competence	Demonstrates Minimal Competence	Demonstrates Emerging Competence	Demonstrates Competence for Internship	Notes
STANDARD I—Data-Based Decision Making and Accountability (NASP STANDARD II)					
1A. Student uses varied methods of assessment and data collection methods for identifying strengths and needs, developing effective services and programs, and measuring progress and outcomes.					
1B. Student demonstrates skills to use in psychological and educational assessments, data collection strategies, and technology resources.					
1C. Student applies results to design, implement, and evaluate response to services and programs.					
STANDARD II—Consultation and Collaboration (NASP STANDARD III)					
2A. Student uses varied methods of consultation, collaboration, and communication applicable to individuals, families, groups, and systems (e.g., teacher and parent consultation, instructional and behavioral consultation, team collaboration).					
2B. Student uses these varied methods (e.g., teacher and parent consultation, instructional and behavioral consultation, team collaboration) to promote effective implementation of services.					
2C. Student demonstrates skills to consult, collaborate, and communicate with others during design, implementation, and evaluation of services and programs.					

(continued)

PRACTICUM CANDIDATE EVALUATION FORM (*continued*)

Performance Indicators (Please place a check mark in the box that indicates current student performance on each indicator identified in the following.)	Does Not Demonstrate Competence	Demonstrates Minimal Competence	Demonstrates Emerging Competence	Demonstrates Competence for Internship	Notes
STANDARD III—Interventions and Instructional Support to Develop Academic Skills (NASP STANDARD IV.1)					
3A. Student uses biological, cultural, and social influences on academic skills; human learning, cognitive, and developmental processes; and evidence-based curriculum and instructional strategies in practice.					
3B. Student demonstrates skills to use assessment and data-collection methods in the evaluation of academic skills.					
3C. Student demonstrates skills to implement and evaluate services that support cognitive and academic skills.					
STANDARD IV—Interventions and Mental Health Services to Develop Social and Life Skills (NASP STANDARD IV.2)					
4A. Student uses biological, cultural, developmental, behavioral, social, and emotional influences on behavior and mental health to promote social–emotional functioning and mental health.					
4B. Student uses evidence-based strategies to promote social-emotional functioning and mental health.					
4C. Student uses assessment and data-collection methods to evaluate social, behavioral, and life skills.					
4D. Student demonstrates skills to implement and evaluate services that support socialization, learning, and mental health.					

(continued)

PRACTICUM CANDIDATE EVALUATION FORM (*continued*)

Performance Indicators (Please place a check mark in the box that indicates current student performance on each indicator identified in the following.)	Does Not Demonstrate Competence	Demonstrates Minimal Competence	Demonstrates Emerging Competence	Demonstrates Competence for Internship	Notes
STANDARD V—School-Wide Practices to Promote Learning (NASP STANDARD V.1)					
5A. Student considers school and systems structure, organization, and theory; general and special education systems; and technology resources in practice.					
5B. Student uses evidence-based school practices that promote academic outcomes, learning, social development, and mental health.					
5C. Student demonstrates skills to develop and implement practices and strategies to create and maintain effective and supportive learning environments for children and others (e.g., completion of required systems change project, presentation of systems change project).					
STANDARD VI—Preventive and Responsive Services (NASP STANDARD V.2)					
6A. Student uses principles and research related to resilience and risk factors in learning and mental health, and services in schools and communities to support multitiered prevention.					
6B. Student uses evidence-based strategies for effective crisis response.					
6C. Student demonstrates skills to promote services that enhance learning, mental health, safety, and physical well-being through protective and adaptive factors.					
6D. Student demonstrates skills to implement effective crisis preparation, response, and recovery.					

(continued)

PRACTICUM CANDIDATE EVALUATION FORM (*continued*)

Performance Indicators (Please place a check mark in the box that indicates current student performance on each indicator identified in the following.)	Does Not Demonstrate Competence	Demonstrates Minimal Competence	Demonstrates Emerging Competence	Demonstrates Competence for Internship	Notes
STANDARD VII—Direct and Indirect Services—Family School Collaboration Services (NASP STANDARD VI)					
7A. Student uses principles and research related to family systems, strengths, needs, and culture in practice.					
7B. Student uses evidence-based strategies to support family influences on children's learning, socialization, and mental health.					
7C. Student uses effective methods to develop collaboration between families and schools.					
7D. Student demonstrates skills to design, implement, and evaluate services that respond to culture and context.					
7E. Student demonstrates skills to facilitate family and school partnership interactions with community agencies for enhancement of academic and social–behavioral outcomes for children.					
STANDARD VIII—Diversity in Development and Learning (NASP STANDARD VII)					
8A. Student considers individual differences, abilities, disabilities, and other diverse characteristics in practice.					
8B. Student uses principles and research related to diversity factors for children, families, and schools, including factors related to culture, context, and individual and role differences in practice.					

(continued)

PRACTICUM CANDIDATE EVALUATION FORM (*continued*)

Performance Indicators (Please place a check mark in the box that indicates current student performance on each indicator identified in the following.)	Does Not Demonstrate Competence	Demonstrates Minimal Competence	Demonstrates Emerging Competence	Demonstrates Competence for Internship	Notes
8C. Student uses evidence-based strategies to enhance services and address potential influences related to diversity.					
8D. Student demonstrates skills to provide professional services that promote effective functioning for individuals, families, and schools with diverse characteristics, cultures, and backgrounds.					
8E. Student demonstrates skills to provide professional services across multiple contexts, with recognition that an understanding and respect for diversity in development and learning and advocacy for social justice are foundations of all aspects of service delivery.					
STANDARD IX—Research and Program Evaluation (NASP STANDARD VII.1)					
9A. Student uses research design, statistics, measurement, varied data collection and analysis techniques, and program evaluation methods sufficient for understanding research and interpreting data in applied settings.					
9B. Student demonstrates skills to evaluate and apply research as a foundation for service delivery.					
9C. Student uses various techniques, in collaboration with others, and technology resources for data collection, measurement, analysis, and program evaluation to support effective practices at the individual, group, and/or systems level.					

(continued)

PRACTICUM CANDIDATE EVALUATION FORM (*continued*)

Performance Indicators (Please place a check mark in the box that indicates current student performance on each indicator identified in the following.)	Does Not Demonstrate Competence	Demonstrates Minimal Competence	Demonstrates Emerging Competence	Demonstrates Competence for Internship	Notes
STANDARD X—Legal, Ethical, and Professional Practice (NASP STANDARD VII.2)					
10A. Student engages in responsibilities consistent with the role of a school psychologist (e.g., assessment, consultation, intervention, evaluation).					
10B. Student uses multiple service models and methods; ethical, legal, and professional standards; and other factors related to professional identity and effective practice as school psychologists.					
10C. Student demonstrates skills to provide services consistent with ethical, legal, and professional standards; engage in responsive ethical and professional decision making; and collaborate with other professionals.					
10D. Student applies professional work characteristics needed for effective practice as a school psychologist, including respect for human diversity and social justice, communication skills, effective interpersonal skills, responsibility, adaptability, initiative, dependability, and technology skills.					

(continued)

PRACTICUM CANDIDATE EVALUATION FORM (*continued*)

Professional Comportment	Below Expectations	Meets Expectations	Above Expectations	
Reflective Practice: Student engages in reflective professional practice to improve skills as practitioner, evaluate individual skills and abilities, and incorporate feedback to change or maintain performance.				
Accountability for Learning: Student is active participant in professional development and learning, seeks feedback and supervision to actively solve problems, and changes performance with feedback and support.				
Professionalism: Student presents self in professional way (appearance, written and verbal communication, and interactions), is timely and responsive, and takes responsibility for own actions.				
Oral Communication: Student has effective oral communication with students, school personnel, parents, and others.				
Promptness: Student is on time to meetings and professional activities; submits work in a timely manner; communicates with others in a prompt manner.				
Flexibility: Student is able to make appropriate adjustments to his or her professional practice when expectations, roles, or responsibilities change or vary.				
Productivity: Student contributes to professional work in the field setting in a meaningful manner.				

(*continued*)

PRACTICUM CANDIDATE EVALUATION FORM (*continued*)

Professional Comportment	Below Expectations	Meets Expectations	Above Expectations	
Enthusiasm: Student demonstrates a positive attitude and an eagerness to engage in professional development in the field.				
Self-Awareness: Student has awareness of own skills and abilities and how these impact his or her work in the field.				
Responsiveness to Feedback: Student responds to feedback in positive way and further integrates feedback into work.				
Problem-Solving Ability: Student demonstrates good critical thinking skills and is able to address problems appropriately when they arise.				
Positive Professional Image: Student takes interest in own professional image and conveys respect and positivity about his or her work in the field.				
Rapport With Staff: Student has developed and maintained good working relationships with school personnel.				
[a]**Is student ready to advance to next level of training (e.g., second semester practicum, internship)**	Yes		No	

[a]If supervisor selects "no," that the student is not ready to advance to the next level of training, a meeting will be held between the director of field training, practicum supervisor, student and other relevant individuals in order to assess the appropriate remediation efforts necessary to support the student. Remediation may include development of an academic development plan (ADP) or referral to the Student Affairs Committee (SAC).

(*continued*)

PRACTICUM CANDIDATE EVALUATION FORM (*continued*)

FEEDBACK/COMMENTS

Areas of greatest strength or competency: _____

_____

_____

_____

_____

_____

_____

_____

Areas of least strength or competency (does not necessarily imply unacceptable or inadequate performance):

_____

_____

_____

_____

_____

_____

_____

_____

_____

Additional comments: _____

_____

_____

_____

_____

_____

_____

_____

PRACTICUM TRAINING PLAN

Student: Date:

Practicum Supervisor:

Practicum Site:

Identify a plan for the completion of university and site requirements (including timelines, resources, and persons involved):

Identify professional goals for the practicum experience:

(continued)

PRACTICUM TRAINING PLAN (*continued*)

Respectfully submitted,

_____   _____
Ed.S. Candidate   Date

_____   _____
Supervising School Psychologist   Date

_____   _____
University Supervisor   Date

CONSULTATION SKILLS CHECKLIST

Rate the consultant on each of the following behaviors using the following scale by circling the appropriate rating:

1 = Skill not demonstrated

2 = Minimal demonstration of skill

3 = Good demonstration of skill

4 = Strong demonstration of skill

	Not Demonstrated	Minimal Demonstration	Good Demonstration	Strong Demonstration
Relationship-Building				
Uses effective nonverbal cues (body movements, vocal cues, personal space) in communication	1	2	3	4
Uses open questions to elicit information	1	2	3	4

(continued)

CONSULTATION SKILLS CHECKLIST (*continued*)

	Not Demonstrated	Minimal Demonstration	Good Demonstration	Strong Demonstration
Uses minimal encouragers (statements and gestures) to facilitate elaboration	1	2	3	4
Paraphrases and summarizes to identify major themes and direct conversations	1	2	3	4
Uses reflection to clarify information	1	2	3	4
Listens to and acknowledges different perspectives	1	2	3	4
Uses a nondeficit approach	1	2	3	4
Models positive communication	1	2	3	4
Points out similar experiences	1	2	3	4
Points out consultee contributions	1	2	3	4
Uses language to unify ("we," "us," "our")	1	2	3	4
Creates opportunities for meaningful roles	1	2	3	4
Reframes to manage conflict	1	2	3	4
Provides structure in process and meetings	1	2	3	4

(continued)

CONSULTATION SKILLS CHECKLIST (*continued*)

	Not Demonstrated	Minimal Demonstration	Good Demonstration	Strong Demonstration
Reads nonverbal language effectively	1	2	3	4
Empowers consultees	1	2	3	4
Problem Identification				
Defines problem behavior in behavioral terms	1	2	3	4
Gathers information about hypothesized antecedent, situation, and consequent conditions	1	2	3	4
Determines important dimensions of the behavior (e.g., how often or severe)	1	2	3	4
Establishes baseline data collection procedures	1	2	3	4
Problem Analysis				
Evaluates and establishes agreement on sufficiency and adequacy of baseline data	1	2	3	4

(continued)

CONSULTATION SKILLS CHECKLIST (*continued*)

	Not Demonstrated	Minimal Demonstration	Good Demonstration	Strong Demonstration
Conducts functional analysis/ discusses antecedent, consequent, and sequential conditions	1	2	3	4
Establishes agreement on goal for behavior change	1	2	3	4
Designs inter-vention plan that addresses antecedent, consequent, or situational conditions to be changed and implementation procedures	1	2	3	4
Treatment acceptability is verified	1	2	3	4
Strategies for treatment integrity are addressed, including measurement tools	1	2	3	4
Establishes data collection procedures	1	2	3	4
Plan Implementation				
Plan implementation is monitored	1	2	3	4

(*continued*)

CONSULTATION SKILLS CHECKLIST (*continued*)

	Not Demonstrated	Minimal Demonstration	Good Demonstration	Strong Demonstration
Training and support for plan implementation are provided, as necessary	1	2	3	4
Plan Evaluation				
Goal attainment is evaluated	1	2	3	4
Plan effectiveness is evaluated	1	2	3	4
Strategies to continue, modify, or terminate the plan are addressed	1	2	3	4
A plan to continue or terminate consultation is established	1	2	3	4

PSYCHOEDUCATIONAL REPORT RUBRIC

Category	Met = 2	Partially Met = 1	Not Met = 0	Rating
Background Information	Reason for referral presents a clear guide for the evaluation and referral questions are offered.	Reason for referral presents a guide for the evaluation.	Reason for referral presents a vague guide for evaluation or is not included.	
	Background information presents a picture of the student and sets up a foundation for understanding his or her strengths and needs.	Background information gives a vague picture of the student or includes excessive or irrelevant information for case.	No background information is provided.	
	Observations are written clearly and in observable terms.	Some vague observations are written.	No observations are written.	

(continued)

PSYCHOEDUCATIONAL REPORT RUBRIC (*continued*)

Category	Met = 2	Partially Met = 1	Not Met = 0	Rating
Data Analysis and Interpretation	Interpretations of data are reasonable and accurate and explain the individual's functioning with all given assessments.	Interpretations of data are accurate and explain the individual's functioning on some, but not all assessments.	Interpretations of data are vague and do not explain the individual's functioning on any assessments.	
	Interpretations of data include an accurate and meaningful discussion of normative performance.	Interpretations of data include a vague discussion of normative performance.	Interpretations of data do not include discussion of normative performance or are inaccurate.	
	Interpretations of data are free of psychometric inaccuracies and/or conceptual misunderstandings.	Interpretations of data have few psychometric inaccuracies and/or conceptual misunderstandings.	Interpretations of data contain multiple psychometric inaccuracies and/or conceptual misunderstandings.	
	Scores from standardized tests are tabled appropriately and easily referenced.	Scores from standardized tests are tabled but are not clearly labeled or easily referenced.	Report includes no tables of standardized test scores.	
Synthesis and Application	Conclusions provide the essential information regarding the student, avoids introducing new data, and offers a summary of strengths and needs.	Conclusions provide important information regarding the student, and offer a summary of strengths and needs.	Conclusions are vague and do not provide much information regarding the student.	

(continued)

PSYCHOEDUCATIONAL REPORT RUBRIC (*continued*)

Category	Met = 2	Partially Met = 1	Not Met = 0	Rating
	Conclusion answers the referral questions/reason for referral and provides recommendations for intervention.	Conclusion answers the referral questions/reason for referral or provides recommendations for interventions.	Conclusions do not answer referral questions or provide recommendation for interventions.	
	Report functions as a problem-solving assessment linking assessment to interventions.	Report makes some vague recommendations that are somewhat based off of evaluation findings.	Report does not link referral concerns to assessment to intervention.	
	Recommendations are realistic and consistent with evaluation findings and provide a guide or resource for implementation.	Recommendations are realistic and consistent with evaluation findings but lack specificity or resources for implementation.	Recommendations are not realistic or consistent with evaluation findings.	
Individualized Educational Program (IEP) Recommendations	Student submits all IEP paperwork consistent with case.	Student submits some but not all paperwork consistent with case.	Student submits no IEP paperwork.	
	Recommendations for potential IEP are consistent with evaluation results and any corresponding team information.	Recommendations for potential IEP are consistent with some of the evaluation results or corresponding team information.	Recommendations for potential IEP are not consistent with evaluation results or corresponding team information.	

(continued)

PSYCHOEDUCATIONAL REPORT RUBRIC (*continued*)

Category	Met = 2	Partially Met = 1	Not Met = 0	Rating
Style, Clarity, and Comm-unication	Report is readable, absent of jargon, consistent, and easy to understand.	Report lacks clarify, uses some jargon or inconsistent in structure.	Report readability is highly compromised due to use of jargon, poor structure, and a lack of clarity in writing.	
	Report is organized, logical, meaningful, and appropriate in length.	Report is somewhat disorganized or inappropriate in length (too short or long) but still provides meaningful structure for case.	Report meaning is highly compromised by organization or length.	
	Content is free of typographical errors and misspellings.	Content has a few typographical errors or misspellings.	Report has several typographical errors or misspellings.	
	Grammar and sentence structure are appropriate.	There are a few errors in grammar and sentence structure.	Report has several errors in grammar and sentence structure.	

Total points for report _____/34

PRACTICUM AGREEMENT FOR SCHOOL PSYCHOLOGY PROGRAM

PLEASE RETURN SIGNED COPY

This agreement is entered into on *[EFFECTIVE DATE]* by and between *[INSERT NAME OF SCHOOL OF PSYCHOLOGY]*, hereinafter referred to as "School" and the *[INSERT NAME OF SCHOOL DISTRICT HERE] School District*, hereinafter referred to as "Site" and *[NAME OF STUDENT]*, hereinafter referred to as "Student."
THE TERM of this Agreement shall extend from *[BEGINNING DATE]* through *[ENDING DATE]*. This experience is to be at least _____ hours of field experience.

WITNESSETH

- WHEREAS, the Site is able to provide supervised field experience for graduate Students in the School Psychology Program at the School
- WHEREAS, this experience would further the professional training of such Students
- WHEREAS, the Site believes the services to be provided by the Students as part of their learning experience would be of benefit to the Site
- WHEREAS, it is to the mutual benefit of the parties hereto that Students of the School use the education facilities of the Site for requisite practicum experience

NOW, THEREFORE, in consideration of the covenants, conditions, and stipulations hereinafter expressed and in consideration of the mutual benefits to be derived therefrom, the parties hereto agree as follows.

RESPONSIBILITIES OF THE SCHOOL

1. The School will arrange the requests for assignments will be made to the Site so that sufficient time is available for the Site to process such assignments. Such official requests from the School Psychology Unit will include sufficient

(continued)

PRACTICUM AGREEMENT FOR SCHOOL PSYCHOLOGY PROGRAM (*continued*)

background information regarding the practicum Student to enable the Site to decide if they wish to accept the practicum Student.

2. The School will provide that only those practicum Students who have been carefully screened and officially admitted into the School Psychology Unit will be permitted to report for a practicum Student placement interview.

3. The School will provide that only those practicum Students who are prepared in advanced School Psychology practice and concentrating in School Psychology will be permitted to report for a practicum Student assignment.

4. The School shall assign a qualified faculty member to supervise all practicum Students, consult with and provide assistance to the Site field instructor.

5. The School will present only those practicum Students who provide evidence of physical fitness and personal integrity. Medically, the practicum Student must be free of communicable diseases, including tuberculosis (a negative TB test result must be provided). In addition, the practicum Student must undergo the required criminal investigation background check as stipulated in the Illinois School Code.

RESPONSIBILITIES OF THE STUDENT

1. The Student will conform to the administrative policies, standards, and practices of the Site, and to the ethical and legal standards of the profession.

2. The Student shall identify himself or herself to the public as a "School Psychology Student" or "School Psychology Trainee."

3. The Student will provide his or her own transportation to the Site.

4. The Student will obtain prior written approval of the Site and the School before publishing any materials relating to the practicum experience.

5. The Student, in collaboration with the supervising school psychologist at the Site, will set times, location, and responsibilities of the practicum experience.

6. The Student will provide the supervising school psychologist with copies of syllabi for courses requiring assignments in the Site.

7. The Student will provide the supervising school psychologist with a copy of the Program's articulated objectives as well as the service learning and practicum requirements.

8. The Student, in collaboration with the supervising school psychologist at the Site and the School faculty, will plan activities in each area included in the Program's articulated objectives.

9. The Student will demonstrate and document a wide variety of competencies, as required for the school psychology credential, and consistent with the Program's articulated objectives and National Association of School Psychologists (NASP) School Psychology Program Standards.

(*continued*)

PRACTICUM AGREEMENT FOR SCHOOL PSYCHOLOGY PROGRAM (*continued*)

10. The Student will NOT provide services beyond the limitations of their competencies.
11. The Student, in collaboration with the supervising school psychologist at the Site and the School faculty, will integrate course requirements in the practicum experience.
12. The Student will obtain a written evaluation of performance from the Site supervisor at least once each semester according to the schedule established by the School. This written evaluation is required prior to posting a grade for the Practicum course.
13. The Student will notify the Site of illness, accident or any other situation which does not allow the Student to meet the prearranged program at the Site.
14. The Student will inform the School of any changes in the on-site schedule.
15. Students and faculty advisors are advised to conduct a thorough investigation of the potential Site to determine any unique or unusual personal safety issues which may be present.

RESPONSIBILITIES OF THE PRACTICUM SITE

1. The Site shall promptly process applications of the practicum Students and notify the School.
2. The Site shall accept only those practicum Students that can be assigned to qualified, capable, and willing field instructors.
3. The Site shall provide practicum Students with the same liability protection for job-related, classroom activities as is provided members of the regular faculty of the Site.
4. The Site shall direct the field instructor on or before the end of the practicum Student's assignment to prepare a final evaluation of the practicum Student using the form provided by the School.
5. The Site shall, whenever possible, assign the practicum Student to a field instructor with a master's degree in School Psychology, a Type 73 certificate, and 3 years experience.

OTHER CONDITIONS OF THE AGREEMENT

1. Race, creed, color, sex, and national origin of said practicum Student shall influence neither his or her assignment by the School or acceptance by said Site.
2. This Agreement may be terminated by either the School or the Site with 90 days prior written notice; unless all three parties agree to earlier termination.
3. The practicum Student shall not be assigned to the high school where he or she has graduated, or be supervised by friends, acquaintances, or relatives.
4. The practicum Student shall have a GPA of "B" or better in content area and assessment.

(continued)

PRACTICUM AGREEMENT FOR SCHOOL PSYCHOLOGY PROGRAM (*continued*)

IN WITNESS WHEREOF, the parties have caused this agreement to be signed in their behalf by their duly authorized representatives effective on the day and year first above written.

FOR THE SCHOOL DISTRICT

School District Representative   **Participating School Principal or Designee**

Signature: _____   Signature: _____

Name (Print): _____   Name (Print): _____

Date: _____   Date: _____

Supervising School Psychologist

Signature: _____

Name (Print): _____

Date: _____

FOR THE _____ SCHOOL OF PROFESSIONAL PSYCHOLOGY

School Psychology Program Chair   **Director of Applied Professional Practice**

Signature: _____   Signature: _____

Name (Print): _____   Name (Print): _____

Date: _____   Date: _____

Student

Signature: _____

Name (Print): _____

Date: _____

INDEX

academic programs evaluation, worksheet for, 77
accountable for learning, of supervisees, 96, 98
assessment, case conceptualization process plan
　development of, 28, 30
　worksheet, 31
　results, interpretation of, 35
　test administration and data collection, 30, 32–34

behavioral consultation, 38
behavioral programs evaluation, worksheet for, 78
behavior intervention plan (BIP), 83
BIP. *See* behavior intervention plan

case conceptualization
　for case study evaluation, 24–37
　in consultation, 37–41
　in counseling, 41–47
　process, 24
　　assessment, 28–35
　　intervention, 36–37
　　referral concern, 27
case consultation, 23
　format worksheet, 26
CASEL. *See* Collaborative for Academic, Social, and Emotional Learning
case manager, purpose of, 63
case study evaluations, 128
　components of, 24
casework
　common types, and termination of, 129–132
CBM. *See* curriculum-based measurement
check-in check-out (CICO), 83
CICO. *See* check-in check-out
CIT. *See* consultants-in-training

cognitive behavior therapy, 45
collaboration
　communication, 145–146
　definition for, 141
　professional competence problems, 149–155
　remediation plans, 155–157
　site development and maintenance, 142–145
　family–school, 85
Collaborative for Academic, Social, and Emotional Learning (CASEL), 81
communication, university and site supervisors, 145–147
comportment issues, resolving, 152–155
consultants-in-training (CIT), 38
consultation
　case conceptualization in, 37–40
　in school settings, termination of, 129
counseling
　case conceptualization in, 41–45
　in school settings, termination of, 129–130
coursework, balancing fieldwork with, 157–158
curriculum-based measurement (CBM), 30

DCT. *See* director of clinical training
developmental models, of supervision, 3, 4
director of clinical training (DCT), 142

Education and Secondary Education Act (ESEA), 71
e-mail communications, 14–15
Effective Social and Emotional Learning Programs—Preschool and Elementary School Edition, 81
enthusiasm, of supervisees, 96, 98
ESEA. *See* Education and Secondary Education Act

Ethical Principles of Psychologists and Code of Conduct, 100
evaluation
    in school settings, termination of, 128–129
    of supervisees, 15–18, 47–49, 66–68, 86, 104–109, 125, 138–140
evidence-based interventions, 36, 37

family–school collaboration, 85
FBA. *See* functional behavior assessment
feedback, orientation to supervision and, 15–18
field site orientation, 7–9
field supervisor, 18
field training communications, 145
flexibility, of supervisees, 96, 98
free and appropriate public education (FAPE), in LRE, 51
functional behavior assessment (FBA), 83

general outcome measures (GOMs), 74
goal-directed teaching activities, stages of, 5–6
GOMs. *See* general outcome measures
grit, 97
group supervision format, 11–13
"groupthink" approach, 153

IDEIA. *See* Individuals with Disabilities Education Improvement Act
IEPs. *See* Individualized Education Plans
IEP team. *See* individualized education program team
independence, of supervisees, 94–99
Individualized Education Plans (IEPs), 41
    development of
        goals, 64–65
        supervisees' role in, 64–66
individualized education program (IEP) team, written and oral reports, 52–53
individual supervision format, 9–11
Individuals with Disabilities Education Improvement Act (IDEIA), 51
individual training plan, components of, 144
information management systems, 59
informed consent, 43
internship planning
    developing a portfolio of work, 121–125
    evaluation of supervisee, 125

preparation, 113–115
requirements for, 111–115
search process, 113, 115
securing, 113
trainee professional development, 115–121
interobserver agreement, calculation of, 34
intervention, case conceptualization process, 36–37

least restrictive environment (LRE), 51
long-term goal-setting activity, 122
LRE. *See* least restrictive environment

mental contrasting, 99
"minimal marking" method, 59
MTSS. *See* multitiered systems of support (MTSS)
multitiered systems of support (MTSS)
    practices, 54, 71
    academic failure prevention
        curriculum, instructional design and delivery, 75
        professional support and development, 79
        screening and monitoring, 74
        Tier 1, 2, and 3, supervision activities for, 75–76
    to promote prosocial behavior, 80–84
    school-based prevention, 84

NASP. *See* National Association of School Psychologists
NASP PREPaRE model, 84
NASP Standards for Graduate Preparation of School Psychologists, define practica, 1
National Association of School Psychologists (NASP), 56, 123
National Certification in School Psychology (NCSP), 123
National Staff Development Council, 79
"No Child Left Behind," 71

ODRs. *See* office discipline referrals
office discipline referrals (ODRs), 82
Olweus Bullying Prevention Program, 84
oral report, 53–55
    in team/IEP meetings, guidelines for, 61

Pendleton method, supervisee feedback for, 17
portfolio development, 121–124
practicum activity worksheet, 95
presenting evaluation results, 60–63
prevention-oriented practices, 80
proactive intern, 94
process developmental models, 4
professional competence, prevent trainee problems of, 149–155
professional development, 79
    goal, 121
    novice level of, 4
    supervision activities for, 79–80
professional relationships activities, termination of, 134–135
professional work characteristics, supervisees, 94–99
proficiencies, 149
psychoeducational report, objectives of, 54

referral concern, case conceptualization process, 27
reflective practice
    of supervisees, 96, 98
    through journal writing, 116–118
    for trainee professional development, 116–117
report writing process, 53–56
    checklist, 57
role expansion, 90–94
rubrics, for self-assessment, 120

sandwich method, supervisee feedback for, 16
school-based behavioral consultation, 38
school-based counseling, termination in, 132
school-based prevention programs, 84
school psychologist-in-training, practicum for, 1
school-wide behavior supports, 81–82
School-wide Positive Behavioral Interventions and Supports (SWPBIS), 82
self-assessment, 120
    trainee professional development, 117–121
self-awareness, of supervisees, 96, 98
self-care
    checklist, evaluation of supervisee, 105–106

plan worksheet, 107–108
    supervisees, 99–104
    supervision activities to support, 100–102
    strategy, 101
session objectives for supervision, 10
site development and maintenance, collaboration
    agreements and partnerships, establishment, 143–144
    building networks for, 142, 143
    relationships for, 142
site supervisors, university and communication, 145–147
    training and support for, 146–149
SMART method, supervisees using, 19
SOAP note. *See* subjective, objective, assessment, and plan note
solution-focused models, 45
solution-focused reports, 54
special education process
    district procedures for, 52
    district services, 66
    IEP team, 52–53
    individual education plan, 64–66
    process, 51–64
    summarizing and presenting results, 53–63
stage-based developmental model, 4–5
stress, of supervisees, 99–104
subjective, objective, assessment, and plan (SOAP) note, 45
    for school-based counseling case, 47
summarizing results, in writing, 53–56
summative evaluation
    of supervisees, 66–68
    of trainee skills, 15
supervisees
    evaluation of, 15–18, 47–49, 66–68, 86, 104–109, 125, 138–140
    independence of, 94–99
supervision, in school psychology, 2–4
SWPBIS. *See* School-wide Positive Behavioral Interventions and Supports

TCSPP. *See* The Chicago School of Professional Psychology
telesupervision, 15

termination
   casework, 127, 130–133
      checklist for, 131
   of consultation, 129
   of counseling, 129–130
   of evaluations, 128–129
   professional relationships and building
      activities, 133–138
   in school-based counseling, 132
   by transition planning creation, 135–139
The Chicago School of Professional
      Psychology (TCSPP), 16
theme-based reports, 54
The National Association of School Psychologists
     (NASP) Model for Comprehensive and
     Integrated School Psychological Services,
     practice domains, 89–94
Tier 2 interventions, 83–84
Tier 3 interventions, 83–84
time management, 120
trainee professional development, internship,
     115–121
   professional goal development, 121
   reflective practice, 116–117
   self-assessment, 117–121
training
   by collaboration, 141–142
      communication, 145–146

coursework, balancing fieldwork with,
     157–158
   professional competence, prevent trainee
     problems of, 149–155
   remediation plans, 155–157
   site development and maintenance,
     142–145
   and support, 146–149
   university and site supervision, 146–149
   in consultation, 39
   plan, development of, 18–19
   programs, practicum for, 1
   skills, summative evaluation of, 15
transition planning creation, termination by,
     135–139
2013 CASEL Guide: Effective Social and
     Emotional Learning Programs—
     Preschool and Elementary School
     Edition, 81

videoconference format, of supervision, 15

wish outcome obstacle plan (WOOP), 99
WOOP. *See* wish outcome obstacle plan
"wrap-around" services, 83
written report
   checklist, 57
   summarizing results in, 53–56